Beyond the Fence Line

THE EYEWITNESS ACCOUNT OF ED HOFFMAN AND THE MURDER OF PRESIDENT KENNEDY

by

Casey J. Quinlan
&
Brian K. Edwards

JFK LANCER
PRODUCTIONS & PUBLICATIONS
SOUTHLAKE, TX

JFK Lancer Productions & Publications, Inc.
401 N. Carroll Avenue, #204
Southlake, TX 76092

JFK Lancer First Edition, October 2008

The goal of JFK Lancer Productions & Publications, Inc. is to make research materials concerning President John F. Kennedy easily available to everyone. Our prime concern is the accuracy of history and the true story of the turbulent 1960s.

For additional copies of this publication, please contact:
Email: orders@jfklancer.com
Web: www.jfklancer.com

For information on Ed Hoffman, see www.jfklancer.com/catalog/ed_hoffman

Printed in the United States
ISBN Number 978-0-9774657-4-3

Beyond the Fence Line

THE EYEWITNESS ACCOUNT OF
ED HOFFMAN AND THE MURDER
OF PRESIDENT KENNEDY

Casey J. Quinlan
&
Brian K. Edwards

"It's easy to imagine an infinite number of situations where the government might legitimately give out false information. It's an unfortunate reality that the issuance of incomplete or even misinformation by the government may sometimes be perceived as necessary to protect vital interests."

THEODORE OLSON, UNITED STATES SOLICITOR GENERAL, WHOSE WIFE, BARBARA, DIED SEPTEMBER 11, 2001.

Contents

Foreword

Jim Marrs

After almost 25 years of investigating and studying the assassination of President John F. Kennedy, imagine my excitement upon learning of a possible witness to the activity behind the wooden picket fence on the infamous Grassy Knoll in Dallas' Dealey Plaza.

Now imagine my consternation to learn that perhaps the most important witness to the assassination had been deaf since childhood and could only communicate by the use of sign language.

Yet a morning in August, 1985, spent with Ed Hoffman convinced me that he was not only honest and sincere in his account of November 22, 1963, but incredibly accurate as well. Any errors or discrepancies in Ed's testimony have been the result of misinterpretations or misunderstandings of his sign language or that of interpreters. His basic account has never varied over the years and everyone who knows Ed vouches for his honesty and integrity.

For me, the Ed Hoffman saga began in the late spring of 1985 as I was completing one of my semi-annual courses on the JFK assassination at the University of Texas at Arlington. I had begun teaching this course in 1976 and continued with it until my retirement at the end of 2006.

A woman attended my class that spring whose deaf parents were friends of Ed and his wife, Rosie. One day in class, she casually mentioned that she knew a man who had witnessed what went on behind the picket fence at the time of the assassination. Needless to say, her statement got my attention.

It took some time to arrange a meeting with Ed, as well as an interpreter. It finally came together on Saturday, August 10, 1985, when all concerned gathered behind the wooden picket fence on the Grassy Knoll. Besides Ed and myself, there was a collection of friends and relatives, both hearing and deaf.

Realizing the importance of Ed's testimony, I was quite cautious and meticulous in my questioning.

Ed aided the process immensely by pantomiming both his actions and the actions of the men he observed. He spared no effort in trying to make me understand completely his story. We would go over questions repeatedly until I felt I understood his meaning.

I am gratified today that, notwithstanding the number of people involved and conditions on that Saturday morning, I was able to get Ed's story nearly correct.

The greatest mistake was a misinterpretation of my question regarding the man Ed saw running behind the picket fence. I asked, "Did he have an overcoat?" The interpreter asked this of Ed using the sign for "coat" which also means "jacket." Ed signed back, "Yes, a nice suit," whereupon the interpreter told me, "It was a nice overcoat." Honest mistakes such as this abound in several interviews with Ed over the years. They have been used to try and discredit his account.

Compared to the incredible amount of detailed information presented by Ed, this mistake in translation was trivial. His descriptions included seeing cars parked along Stemmons, a detail which, while true, went unreported in the news media following the shooting in Dealey Plaza. Ed also accurately described the locations of three Dallas policemen, whose later reports confirmed their locations.

Most impressive to me was Ed's description of a weapon he saw brandished by a Secret Service agent in Kennedy's follow-up car. Ed first said the man held a rifle. But after furthering questions, he used his hands to quite competently describe a weapon with a pistol grip, a forward grip and a handle on top — I knew immediately he meant an M-16 or its civilian model, the AR-15. And, indeed, agent George W. Hickey testified that he had held up an AR-15 as the stricken President was rushed to Parkland Hospital.

Ed then acted out the activities of both the man seen running behind the fence with a rifle and a man who caught the weapon, disassembled it and placed it into a bag before calmly walking away. Ed described the latter as dressed in coveralls similar to that worn by railroad workers and his description of the bag left no doubt that it resembled a soft canvas workman's tool bag.

I joined Ed and his entourage in walking from behind the picket fence to the spot where he stood on Stemmons Expressway. Despite nearly 25 years of growth, it was clear to me that in 1963, Ed had an unobstructed view to the backside of the picket fence. Likewise, a billboard sign some say would have blocked his view, was low enough and far enough to Ed's right to ensure a good line of sight.

With all this confirmation of Ed's details surrounding his experience on November 22, I accepted his account of men behind the picket fence and at the railroad switching box at face value.

It has become the work of Casey Quinlan and Brian Edwards to produce the definitive account of Ed's experience. Hopefully, their meticulous research will put to rest the many efforts — both well-meaning and otherwise — to discredit Ed and his story.

After learning of Ed Hoffman's life, his integrity and his clear view of a man with a rifle on the Grassy Knoll, the reader will more fully understand why Ed's uncle, Dallas Police Lt. Robert Hoffman, even today believes that Ed's life would have been in danger if he had made his story plainly understandable to the authorities in 1963.

This danger would not have come from Lee Harvey Oswald.

By Jim Marrs
April 7, 2008

Preface

Historians, not unlike professional investigators, often must reach conclusions with fragments of evidence and few "hard" clues. They examine what evidence they have, question its relevance to the case, and try to access its validity. Then, after weighing this evidence against what they already know to be true, they formulate tentative answers, which they scrutinize and test. It is important to remember what we often accept as historical "truth" is always being reexamined and questioned with new interpretations and new theories.

History is not an exact science with right and wrong answers. It can be argued there are exact answers to only the unimportant and trivial historical questions. When we ponder these questions and examine the pertinent evidence, even highly trained historians can reach quite different conclusions.

While the interpretations of professional historians may differ, it does not suggest all viewpoints are equally valid. Indeed, just as with any expert testimony, some arguments are more persuasive, more authoritative, or more logical. These stronger arguments are often supported with the most reliable data and hard physical evidence.

This book is designed to help students of the John Kennedy assassination to become better historians and to give them the opportunity to do what historians do, that is, examine the evidence and weight it against what they already know. This is a challenging endeavor and most students may find it difficult. However, with practice and perseverance, they can become successful historical detectives.

Students of history should weigh the available evidence in order to reach informed conclusions, and to argue their positions based on the available evidence. This not only replicates what historians try to do, but it describes what all of us as American citizens must do. Just like historians, we often struggle with incomplete, biased, and contradictory information.

And, just as evidence sometimes leads to different conclusions about important events, we often disagree on issues of contemporary American life. Democratic citizenship, just like history, is hardly an exact science. Instead, it should result in reflective, informed, concerned, and independent decisions for each of us.

Casey and Brian in Dealey Plaza, 2006

The Authors

About the Authors

Casey J. Quinlan was born and raised in Kansas City and has been a high school teacher in Kansas for over 32 years.

Quinlan served in the United States Army with the 9th Infantry as a medical corpsman during the Vietnam War. He earned a Bachelor of Science in Education and a Master's degree in American History from Emporia State University in Emporia, Kansas. He is co-director of Project JFK/CSI Dallas, a student-oriented historical experience for high school and college students.

Quinlan has been the featured speaker at many colleges throughout the Midwest, including the Alf Landon Lecture Series at Kansas State University, the William Allen White School of Journalism at the University of Kansas, and the Johnson County Community College in Overland Park, Kansas.

Quinlan has served as a guest historian for the A&E network, the History Channel, and Oliver Stone's movie, "JFK."

In 1995, Quinlan was named the Outstanding Educator of the Year by JFK Lancer. From 1997, Quinlan has served as an adjunct instructor at Friends University in Wichita, Kansas; Ottawa University in Overland Park, Kansas and Washburn University's Criminal Justice Department in Topeka, Kansas. Today, Quinlan teaches American Government at Marysville High School in Marysville, Kansas.

Brian K. Edwards has been researching the JFK assassination since 1969 and has read over 300 books on the subject. From 1981-1997, he served as a police officer with the Lawrence, Kansas Police Department, and was a senior member of the Department's Tactical Response Team. Edwards received his Bachelor's and Master's degree in Criminal Justice from Washburn University in Topeka, Kansas. From 1996 to 2005, he served as an adjunct instructor for the criminal justice department, with Washburn University, and taught a variety of law enforcement-related courses.

Edwards has lectured on the JFK assassination throughout the Midwest, including the University of Kansas Law School, Washburn University School of Law, Johnson County Community College, and the Alf Landon Lecture Series at Kansas State University. He has served as an adjunct instructor at Friend's University in Wichita, Kansas, Ottawa University in Overland Park, Kansas, and Washburn University in Topeka, Kansas.

Edwards is co-director of Project JFK/CSI Dallas, a student-oriented historical experience. For the past 20 years, Edwards and Quinlan have sponsored student trips to Dallas to study the assassination.

Project JFK/CSI Dallas:
Solving American's Greatest Murder Mystery

President John F. Kennedy was assassinated over 45 years ago in one of the most brutal political murders in the history of the United States. This murder remains an unsolved mystery and has never been subjected to an American criminal court with legal jurisdiction. Casey Quinlan and Brian Edwards have diligently researched the case for the past 40 years.

As high school and university instructors, Quinlan and Edwards have developed a unique workshop for their students. Each student becomes an armchair detective and is challenged to think and search for the truth. Using the current and available technology as a blueprint, each student is provided with all the facts and documentation, and tour the Dealey Plaza crime scene, in an attempt to reach a more logical and reasonable explanation for this murder.

Quinlan and Edwards have created this workshop as an exploratory guide in establishing a more logical and sensible explanation to the events surrounding President Kennedy's murder. This crime is America's nightmare and this workshop is designed to examine the evidence, and establish the truth.

Project JFK/CSI Students in Dealey Plaza

Book Cover Design

On the weekend of November 22, 2007, students from Basehor-Linwood High School in Basehor, Kansas, helped the authors design the cover for this book. We would like to recognize these students for their assistance:

Brook Adams, Jessica Baker, Carley Breuer, Kelly Courtney, Shelby Equels, Leah Gile, Lindsey Johnson, Amanda Koepke, Rebecca Koepke, Katrina Kunard, Nicole Lopez, Taylor McKinley, Sarah Mulford, Alex Oakes, Macyn Sanders, Maigan Snider, Shelby Witt, Brady Blackwood, Brandon Eberth, Matt Gibson, Jeremy Gonzales, Jimmy Goss, Owen Lewis, Brett Martin, Dylan Nigh, A.J. Richardson, Ben Scott, Blake Sneed, Bryson Trowbridge, Austin Walker, Joshua Koepke, Austin Welling, and Shelby Witt.

Acknowledgements

This project could not have been possible without the encouragement and support of Ed and Rosie Hoffman. Their friendship over the past fifteen years has inspired us to make this project a reality. Ed and Rosie have always been willing to discuss the events of November 22, 1963, and how it affected their lives. Ed's recollection regarding his observations that day have remained intact and vivid, considering that the event took place over forty-five years ago. Ed Hoffman would be the first to admit that the aging process has not been kind to him, but his mind and memory are intact.

The authors want to thank Ed and Rosie Hoffman's daughter, Mary Sawyer. In 1989, after reading about Ed's story in Jim Marrs' book, "Crossfire," we were determined to meet and interview this remarkable man. On one of our many trips to Dallas, we drove to Grand Prairie and located Hoffman's Floral. It was after 5 p.m. and the shop appeared to be closed. After knocking on the door for several minutes, we made contact with Ed's daughter, Mary Sawyer.

Without knowing anything about us, or our agenda, Mary arranged to have her dad come to the shop to meet with us. From that moment, we became a part of the Hoffman-Sawyer family.

Mary has always made her parents available to our students without hesitation. Anyone who has met Mary knows she is a loving and caring person who mirrors the upbringing of two wonderful parents. In 1999, at her father's request, Mary donated her father's entire JFK assassination collection to the authors. This material has been an invaluable resource and this project would not have been possible without Mary's trust and support.

Thanks to Jim Marrs and Bill Sloan. Marrs was the first author to research and publish Ed's story in "Crossfire." Mr. Sloan, in his book, "Breaking the Silence," dug deeper into Ed's story and interviewed family members and acquaintances who knew Ed at the time of the assassination.

Ron Friedrich, who as Ed and Rosie's pastor in Grand Prairie, served as editor for Ed's book, "Eye Witness." It was his dedication that got Ed's story on paper which served as a starting point for this project.

Special thanks to Jack White for allowing us access to his vast collection of assassination-related photographs. Mr. White was an invaluable source for many of the photographs that appear in this book.

Debra Conway at JFK Lancer Productions & Publications for her tremendous support and friendship during this project. Also, Sherry Fiester and Clint Bradford for their attention to detail in assisting us in the editing of this book. Finally, Robin Lewis for her technical expertise in making our first book a success.

Rosie, Ed and Mary,
Tyler, Texas 2007

Introduction

"I could very closely examine the head wound, and I noted the right posterior portion of the skull had been extremely blasted. I could literally look down into the skull cavity and see that a third of the brain tissue had been blasted out. "

Dr. Robert McClellan

Introduction

In Dallas, Texas, on November 22, 1963, Virgil "Ed" Hoffman witnessed a historical event. At the time, he had no way of knowing that he was about to witness a political assassination. As he stood on a highway 200 yards west of Dealey Plaza, he saw a man fire a rifle from behind a wooden fence who very likely may have killed President Kennedy. The identity of that man has remained a mystery since that day. Of one thing Ed Hoffman is absolutely certain... *that man was not Lee Harvey Oswald!*

Ed Hoffman is an ordinary man who happens to a deaf mute. In less than one hour after the assassination, Ed had communicated to his dentist, a few friends, his father, and his wife the tragic events he had seen in Dealey Plaza. In order to communicate with others, Ed must rely on his use of handwritten notes, gestures and sign language. Ed communicates on a different level than those who have the ability to hear and speak.

Another matter in his eyewitness account is there is no photographic evidence to verify or deny that Ed Hoffman was where he said he was on November 22. Yet his detailed description of the events prior to the crime and its aftermath has been substantiated by other witnesses and from photographs taken before, during and after the assassination.

We have prepared this book, not to convince the skeptics, but to provide meaningful documentation to the researcher and to the student of history. Our goal is report the documented facts and to offer some linguistic analysis of the problem of sign language transliteration. We invite the reader to examine the presented evidence in order to reach their own conclusions.

Finally, we offer this eyewitness account in response to the published criticism of Ed Hoffman. Ed's critics often cite the same two issues: he has changed his story about what he saw, and his own father did not believe him.

We undertook this project for many reasons. One was to answer those critics and skeptics who declare (without factual data) that Ed Hoffman did not see what he claimed to have seen. Unless Hoffman's critics can turn back time and put themselves in his location, they have no rationale explanation of what one person saw or did not see. There is no denying that something unusual occurred behind the picket fence on top of the grassy knoll. What that something was is open to debate. Who among us can say with absolute certainty that something unusual didn't occur behind the picket fence and that Ed Hoffman didn't see it?

Discounting Ed's story is the same as saying that all the witnesses to the Kennedy assassination are not reliable. How do you choose which witness to accept as credible? Apparently those who served on the Warren Commission knew which to accept as credible. They chose only the evidence which pointed to Lee Harvey Oswald and the Texas School Book Depository. They refused to accept any evidence of shooters, smoke, or additional shots coming from the fence line on the grassy knoll.

Serious researchers and investigators would collect all the available evidence and follow it to a conclusion. Ed's critics, much like the Warren Commission, seem to have the luxury of knowing which information to accept and which to discard.

If Ed Hoffman is not telling the truth, what was or is his motivation?

Is it money?

Ed Hoffman certainly did not become wealthy as a result of telling his story. Ed and his wife Rosie have never been rich, and currently live on social security. He supported his wife as an assembly line worker at Texas Instruments for over 30 years while working part-time at the family floral shop.

Is it fame?

Ed Hoffman is probably not known to anyone outside his family, friends, or assassination researchers.

Is it self-promotion?

Anyone who has the opportunity to meet and talk to Ed Hoffman knows the answer to that question. We challenge the reader to find any evidence that Ed Hoffman ever promoted himself as "The Witness" or profited from his terrible experience of November 22, 1963.

Fortunately for Ed, the critics have begun to be silenced as additional photographs from that day are being discovered and published. Researchers are finding it easier to discover things were just as Ed described them on the day of the assassination:

- There *was* a uniformed Dallas police officer stationed on the railroad bridge over Stemmons Freeway

- Several different cars *did* drive into the parking lot on the west side of the book depository minutes before the shooting

- Unknown people *were* seen on the back side of the picket fence before, during, and immediately after the shooting

- There *was* an encounter between a uniformed police officer and a man in a business suit behind the picket fence immediately after the shooting

- A Secret Service agent *was* standing in the follow-up car and holding a rifle as it passed Ed's location

- The President's head wound as seen by Ed Hoffman from Stemmons Freeway, *was* consistent with the wounds seen by medical personnel at Parkland Hospital within five minutes of the shooting

- A freight train *did* pass north over the triple overpass after the motorcade had traveled through Dealey Plaza

The motivation for this project was to tell Ed's story completely and accurately. We challenge those critics to produce direct evidence which could prove that Ed Hoffman was not standing on Stemmons Freeway on November 22, 1963 between 11:50 a.m. and 12:35 p.m.

In addition, the authors would welcome the opportunity to debate those same "critics" on any issue related to the observations and activities of Ed Hoffman.

Between February and September 1964, members of the President's Commission on the Assassination of President Kennedy, and its appointed counsel, heard testimony from 488 witnesses, and examined nearly 4,000 documents related to the assassination.

On September 24, six weeks before the presidential election, the appointed commissioners arrived at the White House and presented their findings to President Lyndon Johnson. On page 71 of the "Warren Report," the Commission concluded not only had been no conspiracy in the death of President Kennedy, but,

> "…the investigation has disclosed no credible evidence that any shots were fired anywhere other than the Texas School Book Depository Building."

The print and electronic media heralded the Warren Report as the most comprehensive criminal investigation ever undertaken in the history of the United States. This Commission of seven "honorable men" had no authority to keep any testimony, document or physical evidence from the American public. However, many of the transcripts and documents were classified as "Secret," while many more were marked "Top Secret."

Any disclosure of information to the media were always in the form of "authorized releases" and were given directly to the press by the Warren Commission or the Federal Bureau of Investigation, in order to prepare the public for the official explanation that was to come, that Lee Harvey Oswald was the lone assassin and there was no conspiracy, either foreign or domestic.

The government's conduct in concealing the evidence in this case, the power to manipulate the major media outlets by releasing false information, the power to interfere with an honest inquiry, and the power to provide an endless variety of experts to testify in behalf of that power, was openly demonstrated in this case.

Thomas Jefferson impressed upon us the notion that when truth can compete in the free marketplace of ideas, it will prevail. Justice does not occur automatically, we must create it. The concept of justice presents a threat to power and in order for us to make justice come into being we often have to fight power.

It is not too late to bring the truth about the assassination into a court of law, not before a commission of important and politically astute men, but before a jury of American citizens.

Ed Hoffman is the most important eyewitness in the murder of President Kennedy. He should have been embraced for coming forward but instead was crucified by the electronic and print media. He is the only witness who can "speak" to the fundamental events of November 22, 1963. The conspirators were hoping that no one would see the activity behind the picket fence, but someone did. The irony is that the only eyewitness to their activity that afternoon has a hearing disability. In 1989, Jim Marrs wrote,

> Why seek the truth about President Kennedy's death? The answer is simple. Unless we, as a nation, come to a truthful understanding of what happened to our chief elected official in 1963, we obviously cannot begin to correctly understand the events that are affecting us today.

The assassination of President Kennedy was a sudden and violent shift of power in this county. That power, weakened by revelations of corruption and unachieved goals, remains with us today. Few people have shown a willingness to confront this power. Ed Hoffman is one of those people.

We as free citizens deserve and demand the truth behind the murder of our President. The only way to make this country the kind of country it's supposed to be is to communicate to the government that no matter how powerful it may be, we do not accept their findings. One can almost hear the spirit of John Kennedy whispering from beyond the picket fence 45 years later.

"Perception, rather than reality, often times becomes the basic building block of history. We base all our actions, behaviors, and values, on what we perceive to be the truth, even though it may be nothing more than a myth."

Brian K. Edwards

"Faith and trust are essential elements in any belief system. These concepts allow a democratic society to solidify an established pattern of acceptance, through the moral application of truth and justice. It's greatest enemy is deception."

Casey J. Quinlan

We hope you enjoy this book.

Motorcade Route &
Crime Scene Maps

"It has been clearly evident for years that the American public, and the people of the world, do not believe that Lee Harvey Oswald killed John Kennedy. Their belief is well-founded. The evidence is on their side. It is the side of truth."

L. Fletcher Prouty

Dealey Plaza Area Maps, Dallas, Texas

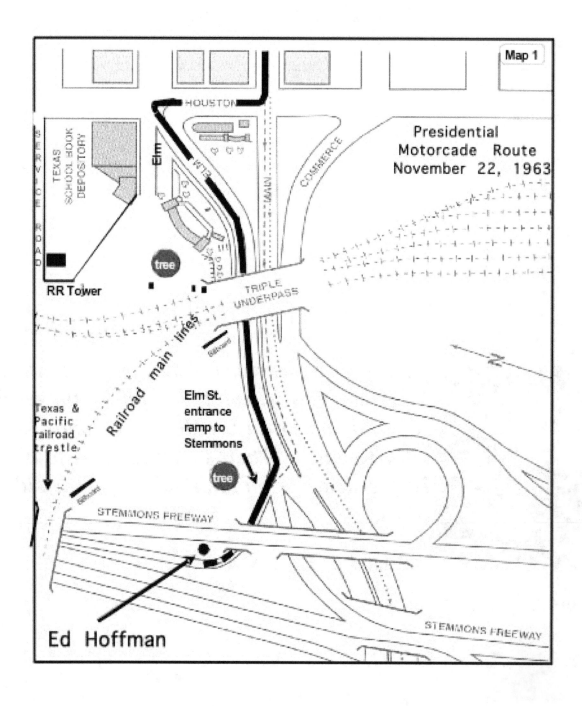

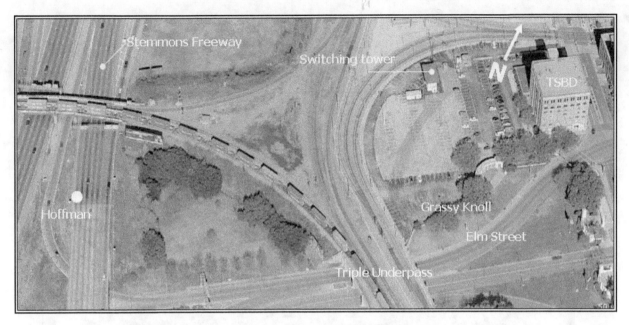

Photo 1: Aerial view of Dealey Plaza, Dallas, Texas with locations noted.

Photo 2: This aerial photo of Dealey Plaza was taken after 1966.

Photo 3: This view of Dealey Plaza looks east from the triple underpass area. The area inside the dotted lines is where Ed Hoffman observed the two men involved in the murder of President Kennedy.

Photo 4: This photo, taken after 1964, looks northwest into the railroad yards. At the time of the assassination, a total of five Pullman cars were parked on the "dead lines" in the rail yard. The black Pullman cars can be seen in the background of many of the photographs taken during the shooting sequence.

Photo 5: Looking southwest into the parking lot on the west side of the book depository. This parking lot was owned and operated by Olan Degaugh, Yard Supervisor Union Terminal Railroad Company, who owned several private parking lots throughout the downtown area.

A. Man in business suit location

B. rail switch boxes location

white vertical line, Yardman location

Z. grassy knoll

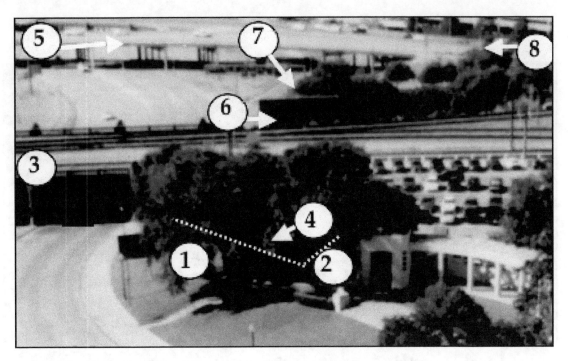

Landmark Map A: Looking West towards Stemmons Freeway
Map Legend:
1. The "grassy knoll"
2. Abraham Zapruder
3. Triple underpass
4. Picket fence
5. Stemmons Freeway (Interstate I-35 North)
6. 'Old Charter' billboard
7. Elm Street entrance ramp to Stemmons
8. Ed's location during the assassination

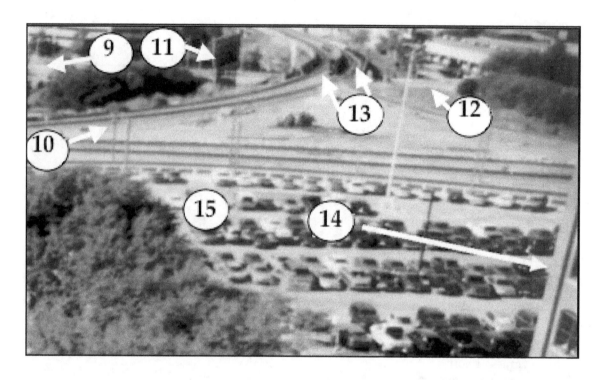

Landmark Map B: Looking west towards the railroad bridge over Stemmons Freeway

Map Legend

 9. Ed's location during the assassination
10. Main railroad lines for in & outbound trains
11. Billboard on Stemmons
12. Northbound traffic lanes of Stemmons Freeway
13. Texas & Pacific railroad trestle over Stemmons Freeway
14. Southwest corner of the Texas School Book Depository
15. Parking lot on west side of book depository.

The Hoffman Identity

*"I saw them shoot the President,
I saw the man who did it!"*

Ed Hoffman

The Hoffman Identity

Virgil Edward Hoffman was the older of two sons born to Frederick and Polly Hoffman on September 20, 1936. At birth Ed had normal hearing, but after turning four years old he contracted an unknown illness that produced a high fever.

The fever caused extensive auditory nerve damage in both ears, causing a complete loss of hearing. When his parents were informed that their son was deaf, they learned sign language to communicate with him.

Ed was sent to Austin to attend high school at the Texas School for the Deaf, two hundred miles from his home. During school breaks and vacations, Ed returned home where his parents included him in all aspects of family life and tried to prepare him for the "hearing world."

During the summers, Ed worked part-time with his father at the floral shop. His father taught him the value of work, the importance of saving money, the virtue of self discipline, honesty, moral integrity and the Christian faith. After graduation in 1952, Ed worked full-time at the shop.

Throughout his life, Ed's relationship with his father was unique among his peers. Ed's father was not only his best friend, but was a mentor, financial advisor, vocational counselor, advocate and protector. Ed's father was his "gate" to the hearing world and it was no surprise that Frederick Hoffman played a more important role in Ed's life beginning on November 22, 1963.

While attending school in Austin, Ed met and fell in love with a young lady named Rosie Jenkins. Four years after graduation, they became husband and wife on November 22, 1956. The newlyweds moved to a small house in the same neighborhood as his parents in Grand Prairie, where Rosie worked part time at the family floral shop. Their only daughter, Mary, was born on January 11, 1958.

In 1960, Ed's father made some inquiries which helped Ed land a job with Texas Instruments in North Dallas. Ed began work in the machine shop and eventually moved into the design department where he worked on some of the newest technology being developed by the company. After thirty-five years of employment with Texas Instruments, Ed retired and currently resides with his wife Rosie in Tyler, Texas.

Project JFK/CSI Dallas has been sponsoring student workshops and tours since 1983. Students spend the weekend investigating the Dealey Plaza crime scene, interviewing eyewitnesses, and researching the case.

Ed and Rosie always made time for students during our weekend trips to Dallas. Many times, Mary would call and ask when we were planning our next trip so she could bring Ed to meet our students. Ed and Rosie loved meeting with the students and always looked forward to our next trip.

Beginning in 2001, Ed's health began to decline but he refused to miss any opportunity to meet with the students and share his story. For several years in a row, Ed was determined to make the trip to Dealey Plaza even though he was confined to a wheelchair.

Webster's dictionary defines the word *hero*, "as a man of distinguished courage or ability, admired for his brave deeds and noble qualities." Ed Hoffman certainly qualifies for this distinction.

Ed is an honest and honorable man, who only wants to tell the truth.

Virgil Hoffman and his father Frederick, 1937

Ed Hoffman age 4

High school graduation, 1952

The Frederick Hoffman family, 1941

Ed Hoffman and Rosie Jenkins

Mr. and Mrs. Ed Hoffman, Wedding day, November 22, 1956.

Ed and Rosie pose as sweethearts in front of Ed's first car.

Rosie, Mary and Ed, 1963

Ed and Rosie Hoffman in front of their home in Tyler, Texas.

Each year on the anniversary of the assassination, Ed and Rosie lay a wreath on the grassy knoll in honor of President Kennedy.

Photos from Hoffman Family Collection

Ed and Rosie with Casey and Brian's students from Kansas City, 1996

Casey, Ed, and Brian, 2007

Photos from authors' collection.

Vantage Point

"Gayle and I were standing along the street watching the parade when what sounded like multiple shots being fired over our heads... I told Gayle to get down...the President was struck in the side of the temple."

WILLIAM NEWMAN

November 22, 1963

While on a mid-morning break at Texas Instruments, Ed Hoffman was chewing the ice from a cup of Dr. Pepper and broke off a portion of one of his teeth. After notifying his supervisor, he left work and drove to his dentist in Grand Prairie.

From the plant in North Dallas, Hoffman traveled through downtown Dallas and exited the highway onto Ross Avenue. He was surprised to see a large gathering of people along the street. He remembered President Kennedy was scheduled to pass through the downtown area that afternoon and decided to delay his trip to the dentist.

To numb the pain of the broken tooth, Hoffman stopped at a convenience store and purchased a package of chewing gum. He packed the chewed gum around the broken tooth, hoping to hold it together until he could reach the dentist's office. Leaving the store, he drove around the downtown area several times looking for a good place to view the motorcade. Unable to find a good location, he and other motorists were directed out of the area by the police. As he drove west on Elm Street, he recalled the local paper indicating that the motorcade would be traveling north on Stemmons Freeway from downtown.

Texas Instruments Plant, North Dallas.

Hoffman took the Elm Street exit out of Dealey Plaza and merged onto Stemmons freeway. As he drove up the entrance ramp to the highway, he noticed that a dozen or more cars were parked on both sides of the highway, and people were standing outside their cars. After parking his 1962 Ford Falcon north of the Texas and Pacific railroad overpass, he walked south along the west shoulder of the freeway and down the Elm Street entrance ramp.

After standing at this location for a few minutes, he decided he would have a better view from an elevated position on top of the overpass. Ed walked up the ramp and onto the freeway and sat on the concrete abutment on the west shoulder of the northbound lane of Stemmons Freeway (Photo 6). He believes he reached this location just before noon.

From this elevated position, Ed was able to see vehicles as they merged onto Stemmons from the Elm Street ramp. Even though he could not see directly into Dealey Plaza, he did notice there were other people standing along Elm Street between the triple underpass and Stemmons Freeway.

In 1963, Stemmons Freeway was a five-lane-wide highway. Each driving lane was a standard thirteen feet wide — 5 multiplied by 13 equals 65 feet. In addition, on each side of the highway, there was one breakdown lane. In 1963, the total width of the freeway was 91 feet. Today, both the north and southbound lanes of Stemmons Freeway are seven lanes wide with no breakdown lanes on either side. The additional lane on the right side of the photo taken in 2008 is for vehicles exiting the freeway (white arrow on Photo 9).

From his elevated position, Ed had an unobstructed view of the area to the east, which included the railroad yard, the west side of the Texas School Book Depository, and the parking lot on the west side of the depository. He was able to see the entire length of the triple overpass and the people standing on it. Hoffman saw one uniformed police officer standing among the spectators on the east edge of the railroad bridge over the underpass. As Hoffman looked around, he noticed one uniformed officer standing on the railroad overpass which crossed over the top of Stemmons Freeway (Photo 12).

According to the duty assignments submitted to the Warren Commission by Assistant Chief of Police Charles Batchelor, two uniformed Dallas police officers, Earle Brown and James Lomax were assigned to this railroad bridge during the motorcade (Lawrence Exhibit # 2, Volume XX pages 489-495. Volume VII, pages 585, 588).

From Hoffman's position (E) in Photo 13, on the west side of Stemmons Freeway to the railroad bridge over the triple underpass (A) was 78 yards; to the east edge of the picket fence (B) was 230 yards; to the middle switchbox (C) was 190 yards. The letter M represents where DPD Officer Joe Murphy told the Warren Commission he stood at the time of the assassination. The distance between Hoffman and Murphy was approximately 85 yards.

As Ed waited for the motorcade, he observed the following:

a) A man in a business suit stood at the backside of the picket fence, facing Elm Street. This man had a stocky build and wore a Fedora-type hat.

b) A second man, yardman, who was tall and slender, stood by the railroad tracks next to the middle of the three switchboxes, (Photo 14). This man wore a hat and some type of coveralls or overalls.

c) Ed saw several men dressed similar to yardman standing on the triple overpass. These men were facing away from him and were leaning on the cement rail overlooking Elm Street.

d) One uniformed police officer (later identified as Officer J. W. Foster) was standing behind these men on the triple overpass at the north end, and a second uniformed officer (later identified as Officer J. C. White) was standing on the west side of the overpass just west of Foster's location.

e) A third uniformed police officer stood at the east end of the picket fence, slightly in front of and facing Dealey Plaza (this officer has not been identified).

f) The man in the business suit walked back and forth between the fence and yard man at least two different times. It appeared to Ed that these two men spoke briefly to each other each time they met.

At about this same time, Ed observed two different cars drive into the parking lot on the west side of the Book Depository. Ed said both vehicles drove into the lot by way of the Elm Street extension.

(TEXT CONTINUED ON PAGE 28)

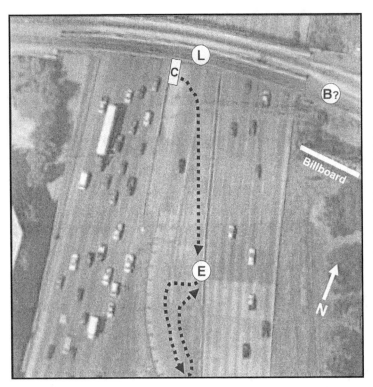

Photo 6: This aerial view of Stemmons Freeway shows where Hoffman, (E) parked his car (C) in relation to the railroad bridge. Letters L and B represents Dallas police officers Lomax and Brown. Both officers were assigned to this location but Officer Brown's exact location during the shooting is unknown.

Photo 7: This photo was taken after 1966. The distance between Ed Hoffman and east end of the picket fence was 230 yards (solid line). In 1963 the top of the Old Charter billboard (arrow) was below the level of the triple underpass and did not block Ed's view from the freeway.

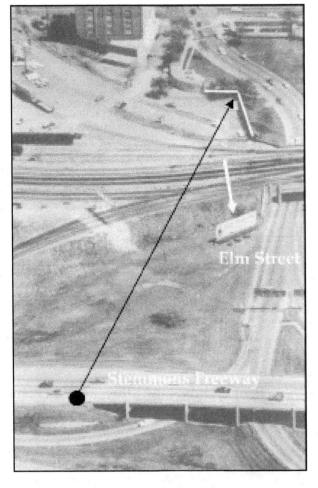

President Kennedy's limousine entered Stemmons Freeway via the Elm Street ramp

Ed Hoffman's location

Photo 8: This photo was taken from atop the railroad bridge looking southeast along Stemmons Freeway.

5 Lanes

1963

7.5 Lanes

2008

Photo 9: Side-by-side comparison of northbound Stemmons Freeway.

Photo 10: Arrow indicates the line-of-sight between Ed Hoffman's location on Stemmons Freeway to the east end of the picket fence. In 1963, this distance was 230 yards.

Photo 11: This photo, taken from the top of the triple underpass, was used by the Secret Service in their investigation of the assassination. This view looks northwest towards Stemmons Freeway.

Photo 12: The distance from Ed's position to the railroad bridge was 78 yards.

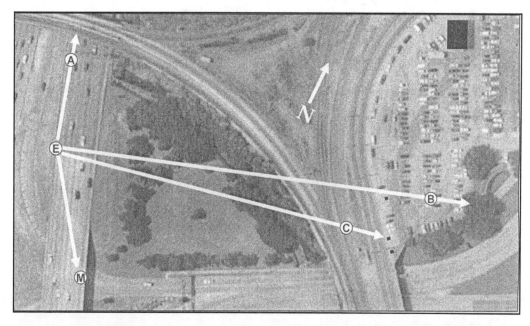

Photo 13: This aerial view represents Ed's position (E) in relation to the railroad bridge (A). the east end of the picket fence (B). and (C) middle switchbox. Position (M) represents Dallas police officer Joe Murphy.

(TEXT CONTINUED FROM PAGE 23)

The first vehicle Ed saw was a white four-door, followed moments later by a light colored Rambler station wagon. The Rambler station wagon shown in Photo 19 is identical to the one seen by Ed Hoffman. Hoffman assumed the drivers were looking for parking spaces and his attention returned to the man in the business suit who was standing behind the fence.

Ed has been asked many times how he was able to distinguish the make of this station wagon from such a distance. He communicated that his best friend, Lucien Pierce, owned a Rambler station wagon exactly like the one he saw driving in the parking lot. For more on the Rambler station wagon, see Chapter 10, *Another Brick in the Wall*.

Lee Bowers, stationed in the railroad switching tower, observed what he described as a "1959 Oldsmobile station wagon" driving in the parking lot about one-half hour before the shooting. Bowers wrote in his affidavit this vehicle circled the parking lot and then left. Was Bowers identifying the same vehicle seen by Hoffman? Did Bowers misidentify the Rambler station wagon as a Pontiac station wagon? Could both men have seen two different station wagons driving in the parking lot? Could Bowers have missed seeing the Rambler station wagon? Did Hoffman not see the Pontiac station wagon?

In Lee Bowers' handwritten statement to the Sheriff's office, he specifically described one of the vehicles he saw driving in the parking lot as a "1959 Oldsmobile station wagon." According to Bowers, after a few minutes this vehicle left the area the via the Elm Street extension. Photo 20 is a black 1959 Oldsmobile station wagon similar to the vehicle seen by Bowers.

Photo 14: This rail switch box was sitting atop an 18″ concrete footing, making it over 6 feet tall. Ed saw yard man disassemble the rifle while standing at this switchbox.

Photo 15: Distance from point A to point B is 26 feet. From point B to point C is 16 feet.

Photo 16: Looking north from the triple overpass. The arrow points to the railroad switching tower where Lee Bowers was stationed on the day of the assassination. The black line represents the steam pipe.

Photo 17: The arrow points to the Elm Street service road. Hoffman saw two vehicles drive into the parking lot via this road.

Photo 18: Hoffman saw the Rambler station wagon drive through the parking lot on the west side of the Book Depository. This vehicle eventually parked near the railroad switching tower.

Photo 19: This is a 1962 AMC station wagon. This type of vehicle is identical to the one seen by Ed Hoffman being driven into the parking lot on the west side of the Book Depository.

Photo 20: This is a 1959 Oldsmobile Super Fiesta station wagon identical to the one seen by Lee Bowers. This type of vehical was driven through the parking lot on the west side of the Book Depository.

Photo 21: The Rambler station wagon seen by Hoffman entered the lot via the Elm Street extension road and parked near the railroad switching tower (white dashed lines). After driving through the parking lot (dashed line) the vehicle eventually parked near the railroad switching tower. After the assassination, the man in the business suit walked over to the Rambler station wagon and got in. The vehicle then drove out of the parking lot along the north side of the Book Depository (dotted line).

Moments before the shooting:

a) A man in a plaid shirt, labeled "P" (dotted black line on Photo 23), stepped around from the north end of the fence, walked up to the man in the business suit "A" and spoke to him for a few seconds.

b) After this brief encounter, the man in the plaid shirt turned and walked back around the east end of the fence and out of Ed's view (solid black line on Photo 23).

c) The police officer, "F" (Photo 23), who had been standing at the east end of the fence, followed the man in the plaid shirt as he walked around the east side of the fence.

d) The man in the business suit, "A," walked over to the yard man, "B," who stood by the middle switch box. The man in the business suit appeared to speak to yardman for a few seconds, and then returned to his original position behind the fence (Photo 24).

e) Yard man bent over at the waist and appeared to be working on something near his feet. He stood with his back against the middle switchbox (Photo 15).

f) The man in the business suit, now standing at the fence, bent over, then straightened up, and looked over the fence towards the street.

g) Ed saw a puff of smoke near where the man in the business suit was standing and believed this man was smoking a cigarette.

h) The man in the business suit turned ninety degrees to the fence and was now facing Hoffman's position. The man in the business suit was holding a rifle. This man carried the rifle with both hands, and held the weapon against his chest as he ran towards yardman.

i) The men on the triple overpass now appeared to be engaged in more animated discussion, and were looking and pointing towards the fence. Hoffman assumed that from their position that they could see the side of the fence that faced Elm Street and that they also saw the same puff of smoke he had observed.

g) The man in the business suit stopped running and tossed the rifle underhanded over a steam pipe that served as a barrier between the parking lot and the train tracks (Photo 24). This steam pipe ran the length of the triple overpass and was about four feet above the ground.

h) Yard man moved towards the man in the business suit and caught the rifle with both hands. Yardman stepped back and stood with his back against the middle switchbox. Yardman bent over at the waist and broke the weapon in two separate pieces and placed them into a soft tool box/bag.

i) Yard man walked briskly north along the railroad tracks away from the triple overpass carrying the box/bag in his hand (Photo 25).

j) The men on the triple overpass stayed on the bridge and continued to point towards the area of the fence and their gestures became more animated.

k) The man in the business suit then turned and walked casually back toward the north end of the fence (Photo 26).

l) A police officer ran from the west end of the triple overpass to the east side. At this point, none of the men on the bridge ran towards the parking lot, but Hoffman saw some of the men pointing towards the grassy knoll.

m) The lead engine of a slow moving freight train appeared at the south end of the triple overpass and was heading north. At this point, Ed lost sight of yard man because of the people that were now running into the parking lot. The men on the triple overpass were still in view and some began to move towards the parking lot.

n) A uniformed police officer, "P" (Dallas police officer Joe Marshall Smith), came around the east end of the fence and confronted the man in the business suit (Photo 26). Ed saw the policeman point his pistol directly at the man in the business suit (This is *not* the same officer Hoffman saw earlier standing at the east end of the fence, that officer was not wearing a hat).

o) The man in the business suit immediately held both arms out to his side, as if to say, "It wasn't me, I have nothing." The man in the business suit reached inside his suit coat and showed something to the officer. Hoffman assumed it was some type of identification because the officer holstered his pistol and both men mingled with the crowd coming around both sides of the fence.

p) At this time, the lead engine of the freight train was moving north across the triple overpass. The man in the business suit walked over to the Rambler wagon and got in on the passenger side, the Rambler station drove out of the parking lot along the north side of the depository. Hoffman last saw this vehicle as it made a right turn onto Houston Street.

Photo 22: This is the railroad switching tower where Lee Bowers was stationed on the day of the assassination. This building is 100 yards north of the picket fence.

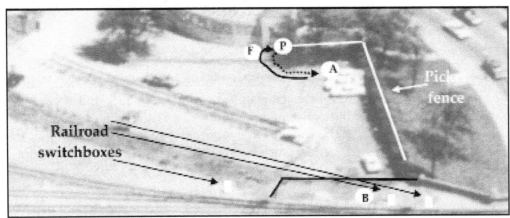

Photo 23: From his position on Stemmons Freeway, Hoffman watched the movements of four different men behind the picket fence — the man in the business suit (A).. a uniformed police officer (F). a man in a plaid shirt (P). and yardman (B).

Photo 24: Ed saw the man in the business suit walk to yardman and return to the area behind the picket fence. The steam pipe (black line) represents the steam pipe that separated yardman and the man in the business suit.

Photo 25: Ed saw the man in the business suit fire the rifle towards Elm Street. A puff of smoke drifted out from the fence where the man in the business suit stood. The man in the business suit (A) turned 90 degrees and sprinted down the fence line in the direction of the railroad switch boxes. The man in the business suit stopped suddenly and tossed the rifle to yardman (B). After catching the weapon, yardman stepped around to the north side of the middle switchbox and broke the weapon into 2 pieces. After putting the pieces into a tool box/bag, yardman casually walked north along the tracks and out of the parking lot.

Photo 26: Ed saw a uniformed police officer (P) confront the man in the business suit (A) in the parking lot.

THE STEAM PIPE

The presence of the steam pipe in the area near the triple overpass is further proof that Ed Hoffman's observations were correct. This steam pipe ran the entire length of the triple overpass and was anchored into the concret pillars. The pipe was approximately 30 inches off the ground and was attached to the east side of the triple underpass by metal brackets. The witnesses who stood on top of the underpass as the motorcade passed below would have been standing very close to the steam pipe. This pipe originated south of the triple underpass. Several witnesses who climbed the picket fence near the north end of the underpass mentioned the steam pipe in their testimony.

The termination point for this pipe was directed into the ground 30 feet north of the underpass. One possible explanation for running the steam pipe on the top of the triple underpass had to do with vehicle clearance. The clearance for the cars traveling through the underpass is 14 feet. If an 8-inch pipe was added, the clearance would only be 13.3 feet. This would restrict the types of vehicles that could pass through the underpass. It was then more practical to run the pipe over the top of the triple underpass, securing it to the concrete support columns along the east side railing.

The importance of the steam pipe to this case is that Hoffman saw the man in the business suit stop suddenly as he ran towards yard man. The man in the business suit would have wanted to get rid of this evidence quickly and his only options were to step over the pipe (on the day of the assassination, the pipe was 30 inches off the ground), crawl under the pipe or go around the pipe. In order to get rid of this damning evidence, the man in the business suit simply stopped at the pipe and tossed the rifle to the yard man and walked away.

Since Ed Hoffman had never had an occasion to walk in the parking lot on the west side of the Book Depository, he had no knowledge of the steam pipe, its purpose, where it originated and terminated. In addition, Hoffman did not know the steam pipe created a physical barrier between the parking lot and the railroad tracks. Hoffman only knew that something made the man in the business suit suddenly stopped running and toss the rifle to yardman who stood six to eight feet away.

How did the men on top of the triple underpass not see yardman at the middle switchbox? The design of the top of the underpass itself is one reason. The answer can be seen in Photo 27. Regardless, if he had been seen, the men on the overpass may have assumed he was just another railroad employee. The photographer who took this picture stood several feet west of the bridge railing. Note none of the three switchboxes are visible in the photograph. As the witnesses stood against the east side of the bridge, it is entirely possible that their view to the north was blocked by the raised concrete support posts of the top of the underpass. Additionally, these witnesses were watching the President and had no reason to look elsewhere.

Photo 27: Commission Exhibit 2214 shows how the steam pipe was attached to the triple overpass at the time of the assassination (arrow). Officer Foster stood on this track switch box (circle) during the assassination.

Photos 28 & 29: This view of the north end of the top of the triple underpass looks east into Dealey Plaza. On each of the concrete support posts along the east railing of the underpass, the bolt holes are still visable where the brackets held the steam pipe. Measuring from the center of these two holes, the authors were able to determine the steam pipe was thirty inches above the ground. The photo on the right was created to show the height of the pipe as it was on November 22, 1963.

Gate in fence
above drainage pit?

Photo 30: This photo, taken sometime after 1966, shows the steam pipe in relation to the picket fence. The pipe acted as a barrier between the parking lot and the railroad tracks to the west. When this photograph was taken, the pipe had been moved closer to the picket fence and had been raised from its original height of 30 inches.

Photo 31: Sometime between November 22, 1963, and when Mark Lane filmed the sequence with Sam Holland, the steam pipe had been raised from its original height of thirty inches.

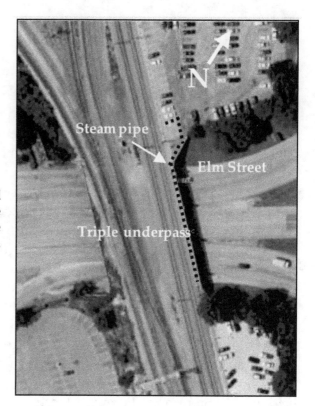

Photo 32: This aerial view of the triple underpass and the parking lot looks north into the parking lot. The black dotted line represents the steam pipe along the east side railing of the top of the underpass.

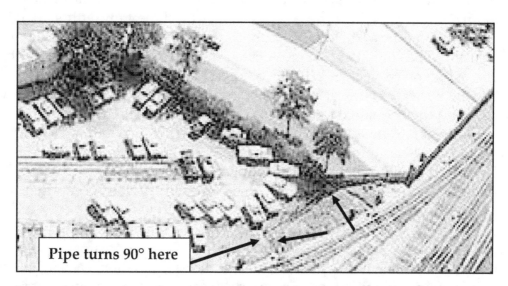

Pipe turns 90° here

Photo 33: The arrows point to the steam pipe separating the west end of the parking lot with the railroad tracks. The steam pipe terminates underground near the railroad tracks. According to Ed Hoffman, the man in the business suit stopped running when he reached the pipe and tossed the rifle over the pipe to yardman.

THE SECRET SERVICE AND THE RIFLE

The President's limousine passed underneath Hoffman's location as it proceeded up the entrance ramp onto Stemmons Freeway (Photos 35 and 36). Hoffman's turned his attention away from the activity behind the fence to the President's car as it came into his view. The limousine was moving slowly enough up the Elm Street on ramp that Hoffman could look directly down into the car from his elevated position on the overpass.

While the vehicle negotiated the entrance ramp, Hoffman was able to make out each of the occupants, but his attention was focused solely on the President. President Kennedy was on his left side and was lying across the rear seat with his head on the left seat (Jacqueline Kennedy's original position during the motorcade). Mrs. Kennedy was kneeling on the floorboard and facing the back of the car (the switch in positions occurred when she crawled out onto the trunk while the car was still in Dealey Plaza). Hoffman saw Mrs. Kennedy shaking the President with her left hand in a futile attempt to revive him.

Hoffman saw one man standing in the president's limousine holding the President and Mrs. Kennedy down. His most vivid memory of that moment was the large gaping wound on the right rear portion of the President's head. Hoffman recalled, "Behind right ear, fist-sized hole, blood covered back seat."

Hoffman turned towards the uniformed police officer stationed on the railroad bridge over Stemmons Freeway. Hoffman began running north along the shoulder of the highway, waving his arms in an attempt to get this officer's attention. Just then the Secret Service follow-up car accelerated up the entrance ramp behind him. As this car passed him on the ramp, Hoffman saw a man standing in the vehicle holding a rifle. This man pointed the weapon directly at him as the car accelerated up the entrance ramp.

Hoffman said he froze in place and didn't move until several vehicles sped past his location. Hoffman described the weapon as "A machine gun with something on the bottom." The authors showed Hoffman a photo of an AR-15 assault rifle with an extended magazine. Without hesitation, he communicated this weapon was identical to the one that was pointed at him on November 22, 1963 (Photo 37).

After the Secret Service car passed his location, Hoffman looked back towards the Plaza to see if he could locate the man in the business suit. The freight train was moving slowly on the tracks from south to north (right to left from Hoffman's point of view). Hoffman could only see through the spaces between the moving train cars. Before the engine of the freight train completely blocked his view of the parking lot, Hoffman saw the man in the business suit walk over to the green Rambler station wagon that was parked near the switching tower.

The man in the business suit got in the Rambler on the passenger side and the vehicle drove out of the parking lot along the north side of the Book Depository.

During the Secret Service's investigation of the assassination, each agent assigned to the Presidential detail submitted written reports describing their actions as it related to the shooting.

Agent George Hickey's report stated, "I then reached down, picked up the AR 15, cocked and loaded it and stood part way up in the car and looked about."

In a second report written by Agent Hickey states,

"I reached to the bottom of the car and picked up the AR 15 rifle, cocked and loaded it, and turned to the rear…I kept the AR 15 rifle ready as we proceeded at a high rate of speed to the hospital."

Secret Service Agent Jack Youngblood, riding in Vice-President Johnson's car directly behind the follow-up car wrote, "…observed Agent Hickey in the Presidential follow-up car poised on the car with the AR-15 rifle looking towards the buildings."

Secret Service Agent Glen Bennett, riding in the follow-up car wrote, "I had drawn my revolver when I saw S/A Hickey had the AR-15."

Secret Service Agent William McIntyre wrote in his report: "Most, if not all the agents in the follow-up car had drawn their weapons, and agent Hickey was handling the AR-15."

After the Secret Service car had passed Hoffman's location, and after the man in the business suit left in the Rambler, Hoffman continued running to his car. He communicated to the authors, "I had to get back there, I saw the man who shot JFK." Since the Dallas police had set up a roadblock behind where Hoffman had parked his car, he was able to drive across all five lanes of Stemmons Freeway, and exited at Continental Avenue (Photo 45).

Five Dallas police motorcycles officers were assigned to stop northbound traffic just south of the railroad bridge. The point where the railroad bridge crosses over Stemmons Freeway is 95 yards south of the Elm Street entrance ramp.

Photo 34: Location of Ed Hoffman (white circle), police officer on the railroad bridge (black circle), and the route taken by the motorcade (white arrow).

Photo 35: This is the view Ed Hoffman had while standing and sitting on the west side of Stemmons Freeway. This elevated position is approximately 15 feet above the Elm Street entrance ramp onto northbound Stemmonds Freeway.

Elm Street ramp to northbound Stemmons freeway

Hoffman's location during the assassination

Photo 36: This photo, taken by the authors, looks southeast from the railroad bridge over Stemmons Freeway. Hoffman stood, sat on the west shoulder of the northbound lanes of the freeway as the president's limousine passed underneath. From this elevated poisition, Hoffman was able to look down into the open limousine.

Photo 37: Colt Firearms AR-15 assault rifle with extended magazine.

Photo 38: This is a cropped version of a photograph taken by Mel McIntire showing the President's limousine approaching the Elm Street entrance ramp. The barrel of a long gun can be seen in the Secret Service follow-up car (arrow).

Photo 39: In this close-up of photo 38, the barrel of the assault rifle can be seen.

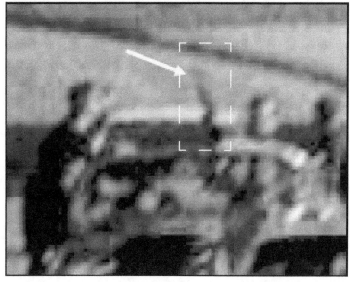

Photo 40: Agent Hickey is holding the AR-15. The arrow points to the tip of the rifle barrel.

Photo 41: This is a close-up of photo 40. The barrel of the AR-15 is clearly seen behind the head of Secret Service agent William McIntyre.

THE POLICE ROADBLOCK ON STEMMONS

The motorcade that traveled from Love Field Airport through the streets of Dallas was made up of twenty-six vehicles containing a variety of dignitaries and political officials. The Dallas police department supplemented the motorcade with seven different groups of motorcycle officers. At the direction of the Warren Commission, Assistant Chief of Police Charles Batchelor prepared a mulit-page document detailing where each Dallas police officer was stationed during the President's visit to Dallas. This document was turned over to the Warren Commission and marked as Commission Document 81.1. Commission Documents *were not* included as part of the 26 volumes on the investigation into the President's assassination.

The first vehicle in the presidential motorcade was designated the "Advance Car." This vehicle, driven by Dallas police Captain P. Lawrence, was assigned to drive ahead of the procession by one-half mile and to ensure the roadway remained clear.

The next vehicle in the motorcade was designated the "Pilot Car." This vehicle was driven by Deputy Chief George Lumpkin. In the vehicle with Lumpkin were two Dallas police detectives, a military officer, and a member of the local democratic organizing committee.

The first group of police motorcycles was designated as the "Advance Unit." Riding in this three-man detail three-to-four blocks ahead of the motorcade were Sergeant S. Bellah and Officers J. Garrick and G. McBride. Two officers from this group, Garrick and McBride, were assigned to the roadblock on Stemmons Freeway. All three officers rode west on Elm and out to the freeway to set up the roadblock.

The next group of motorcycle officers were designated the "Lead Motorcycles." This group of five officers was under the direction of Sergeant S. Ellis who rode with Officers L. Gray, E. Brewer, W. Lumpkin, and H. Freeman. These officers were originally assigned to ride five abreast one to two blocks ahead of the presidential vehicle and would keep the spectators off the streets as the President passed by.

As the motorcade traveled west on Main Street the large crowds prevented these officers from riding five across. Sergeant Ellis directed his officers to ride single file between the curbs and the vehicles trying to keep the crowds on the sidewalks.

According to Commission Document 81.1, by pre-arrangement, Officers Brewer and Freeman "cover Stemmons Freeway traffic lanes to the rear of escort to prevent any vehicles from passing Presidential party." When the last car in the motorcade passed the roadblock, all five motorcycle officers assigned at the roadblock, Bellah, Garrick, McBride, Brewer, and Freeman, would fall in behind and follow the motorcade to the Trade Mart.

To determine when the roadblock on Stemmons Freeway was actually initiated, the authors examined two different versions of the transcripts for the Dallas police radio communications for November 22, 1963. In either of the sets of documents examined, Sawyer Exhibit A, (Hearings and Exhibits, Volume 21, pages 389-397), and Commission Exhibit 290, the authors found no evidence that the order to stop traffic on Stemmons was communicated over police radio channels 1 or 2.

Commission Document 290 is a typed transcript of the radio communication for Dallas police channel 2, prepared on December 3, 1963 by Sergeant G. Henslee, who was the police dispatcher supervisor. This document was submitted to Chief Jesse Curry, who then forwarded it to the Warren Commission. The opening states,

> The following was recorded on Channel 1 from 10:00 am to 5:00 p.m.. This report includes pertinent transmission prior to the arrival of the President's plane, progress of the motorcade, the shooting, and the escort to Parkland Hospital.

Regardless of at what time the roadblock was begun, we do have on record that traffic was being held back after the assassination. The first radio traffic between any of the motorcycle officers at the roadblock and police headquarters came from Sergeant Bellah (radio 190) when he radioed Sergeant Henslee (radio 531) at 12:34 p.m.,

> **190-531:** You want me to still hold traffic on Stemmons until we find out something?

Sergeant Henslee did not respond to Bellah due to the high volume of other officers calling in to police headquarters asking for information and direction. At 12:40 p.m., Sergeant Bellah calls into headquarters again,

> **190-531:** I've got myself and five motorcycle officers holding traffic on Stemmons, do you want me to release traffic or hold it?

Sergeant Bellah advised the police dispatcher that he and five other motorcycle officers (Brewer, Freeman, Garrick, Gray, and McBride), are still at the roadblock on Stemmons Freeway.

Sergeant Henslee responded,

> **531-190:** Release traffic and report code three to Elm and Houston

On December 5, 1963, Sergeant Henslee prepared a second version of the radio communication of channel 1. This document was submitted to Chief Curry who forwarded it to the Warren Commission who designated it as Commission Document 291. This document was entitled, "Transcript of Radio Log. Shooting of President Kennedy. Shooting of Officer Tippit. November 22, 1963."

This set of transcripts only includes radio traffic directly related to the shooting of President Kennedy. Sawyer Exhibit A (Volume 21, pages 388-397) and Sawyer Exhibit B (Volume 21, pages 398-400) are exact copies of Commission Documents 290 and 291, except both Commission Documents has handwritten notations denoting the officer's names and their police radio numbers. Commission Exhibit 1974, (Volume 23, pages 832-940) is the most complete version of communication from Police Channel 1 between the dispatcher, supervisors and patrol officers. The officer's names and radio numbers are typed on this document.

After exiting Stemmons Freeway behind the vehicles assigned to the motorcade, Hoffman communicated it took him nearly one-half hour to travel from Continental Avenue to Elm Street. By now the police were directing all vehicular traffic out of Dealey Plaza by way of Elm Street. Hoffman drove out of downtown and headed towards Grand Prairie.

Before going to the dentist to have his tooth repaired, Hoffman stopped at a body shop in southwest Dallas and contacted Lucien Pierce (Photo 47). Pierce had known Ed for several years and like Ed, was also deaf. Hoffman burst into the shop and excitedly told his friend what he had just witnessed in Dealey Plaza. The hearing employees had no idea what Hoffman was communicating to his friend. His animated sign language, his emotional expressions, and his unintelligible vocalizations amused them. When the shop manager came in and told the other employees about the radio broadcast of the shooting in Dealey Plaza the room suddenly fell deadly silent.

Hoffman left the body shop and drove to the family floral shop and proceeded to communicate to his father, Frederick Hoffman, what he had seen in Dealey Plaza. Ed told his father about seeing the man behind the fence shooting the rifle, and of seeing the wounded President and about the man pointing a rifle at him. Hoffman recalled later that he told his father, "I saw them shoot JFK, I saw who did it!" His father, puzzled by his son's sudden appearance at the flower shop seemed to be more interested in why his son was not at work. Ed remembers that his father was quite angry and ordered him to go the dentist and they would finish the conversation later. Frustrated and in pain, Ed left the floral shop without telling his father the specific details of the actions of the man behind the fence.

Hoffman headed to east Dallas and arrived at Dr. Charles Zawicki's office sometime between 3 and 4 p.m. While in the waiting room, he wrote notes to the other patients, attempting to describe the events he had observed in Dealey Plaza. Since there was no radio playing in the office, the other patients had no idea what Hoffman was trying to tell them.

While in the dentist's chair, Hoffman scribbled notes and handed them to Dr. Zawicki trying to explain where he was and what he saw. Someone in the office turned on a radio and Dr. Zawicki left the examination room to listen to the news bulletins about the shooting.

When the doctor came back into the exam room, he wrote a note telling Hoffman that the news reporters were saying President Kennedy was dead from a gunshot wound. Hoffman tried to communicate that he already suspected the President was dead after seeing the large hole in his head.

The dentist's office fell silent and now everyone gathered around the radio listening to the news accounts of the tragedy. Hoffman recalled the simple tooth repair took over an hour because Dr. Zawicki kept leaving the room to listen to the radio. While Dr. Zawicki worked on his tooth, Hoffman was anxious to leave and get back to his father and tell him what Dr. Zawicki had heard over the radio.

When he returned to the floral shop, Ed's father had already heard the news broadcasts telling of the shooting. Ed asked his father to call the authorities — or at least his uncle so Ed could tell him what he observed. Frederick told Ed, "You go home. The police are busy now. Let them do their jobs."

Ed eventually went home finding his wife, Rosie, watching the television. There was no closed caption capability for the deaf at that time, but Rosie understood enough to know the President had been shot. Ed told her, much to her surprise, that he had been there, and he had seen the man who shot the President.

Photo 42: This aerial view shows the railroad bridge over both north and southbound traffic lanes of Stemmons Freeway (arrow) The white dotted line designates where five Dallas motorcycle officers set up the roadblock. The white dot represents where Ed Hoffman parked his vehicle along the west shoulder of Stemmons Freeway.

Photo 43: This frame from the Zapruder film shows the three motorcycle officers of the Advance Unit. Officer Garrick and Sergeant Bellah are making the left turn onto Elm Street. Officer McBride is at the far right (arrow).

Photo 44: Mary Moorman's first photo of the motorcade shows Officer McBride traveling west on Elm Street. The south side of the Texas School Book Depository is in the background.

Photo 45: This photo, taken from the west shoulder of Stemmons Freeway, looks north towards the railroad bridge (black arrow). When Ed Hoffman parked his car under the bridge, he saw one uniformed police officer standing on the bridge. Because Hoffman had parked his car ahead of the police roadblock, he was able to drive across all five lanes of traffic and exit at Continental Avenue (white dashed arrow).

Ed and Rosie watched the news on television. He was puzzled by focus of the media's attention on the Texas School Book Depository. Why are they looking at the building he wondered? Ed remembers telling Rosie, "That's not where the man shot the gun!"

Frustrated, Ed left home and drove back to the flower shop to plead with his father about calling the police. Frederick told Ed that they had already arrested one man, and would, no doubt, eventually catch the other.

Later that evening, images of Lee Harvey Oswald appeared on the television. Ed bolted from his chair saying, "No, that's not him! That's not the man I saw!" The Hoffman's were celebrating their 7th wedding anniversary that day and had made plans but instead, Ed drove Rosie out to Stemmons Freeway and showed her where he stood when the President was shot.

Ed parked his car along the shoulder of the freeway, just as he had done earlier that afternoon. They walked to where Ed had stood during the assassination. Ed told Rosie what he had seen and pointed in the direction of the railroad yard.

A passing motorist stopped, perhaps thinking the Hoffman's had car trouble. The motorist did not understand sign language, and Ed courteously gestured that they did not need any assistance. The man persisted in offering to help the couple. Ed and Rosie became uncomfortable with the presence of this nosy stranger, and hurried back to their car and drove home. To this day, Ed and Rosie feel that this man's actions and persistence was unusual. He did not act as someone who wanted to help a stranded motorist, but more like someone trying to obtain information.

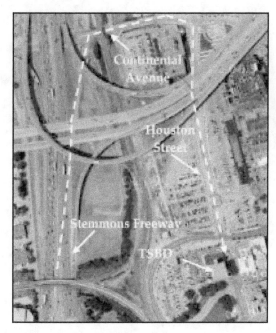

Photo 46: The dashed line indicates the route taken by Ed Hoffman after exiting Stemmons Freeway.

Photo 47: This undated photo is of Lucien Pierce. Hoffman stopped at Pierce's place of employment before returning to the floral shop.

Photo 48: Hoffman's Floral shop, Grand Prairie, Texas.

Lost in Translation

"American Sign Language (ASL) is a complete, complex language that employs signs with the hands and other movements including facial expressions and postures of the body."

NATIONAL INSTITUTE OF DEAFNESS

AMERICAN SIGN LANGUAGE

American Sign Language is the first language of many deaf North Americans, and one of several communication options available to deaf people. American Sign Language is the fourth most commonly used language in the United States.

In spoken language, the different sounds created by words and tones of voice are the most important devices used to communicate. Sign language is based on the premise that sight is the most useful tool to a deaf person has to communicate and receive information. Thus, American Sign Language uses hand shape, position, and movement, body movements, gestures, facial expressions, and other visual clues to form its words. Like any other language, fluency in ASL happens only after a long period of study and practice.

Even though ASL is used in America, it is a language completely separate from English. It contains all the fundamental features a language needs to function on it own — it has its own rules for grammar, punctuation, semantics and sentence order. ASL evolves as its users do, and it also allows for regional usage and jargon. Every language expresses it's features differently, ASL is no exception. Whereas English speakers often signal a question by using a particular tone of voice, ASL users do so by raising the eyebrows and widening the eyes.

Just as with other languages, specific ways of expressing ideas in ASL vary as much as ASL users themselves. ASL users may chose from synonyms to express common words.

There are two language difficulties which have interfered with Ed Hoffman's attempts to communicate his testimony clearly and accurately. The first issue relates to the grammar of American Sign Language (ASL), and the second is the grammar of English.

American Sign Language and English are two uniquely different languages. Sign language is not just another form of English and most people unfamiliar with ASL are unable to appreciate the differences. As with any two languages, there is rarely a "one for one" correspondence between the vocabulary of English and American Sign Language. Just as one English word, such as *right*, can have multiple meanings, depending on the context, an interpreter may have difficulty choosing the precise English word or phrase to express the intended meaning of a particular sign or set of signs.

Some expressions in American Sign Language may have a general, ambiguous meaning, while the English equivalents can only express a specific, narrow meaning. For example, the interpreter who worked for author Jim Marrs signed the general ASL word, *coat* for the specific English word *overcoat*. Ed thought she was referring to the gunman's *suit coat*. That misunderstanding led to an often quoted interpreter error in Marrs' book.

The opposite happens as well. While a word in English can express a general word, American Sign Language requires a specific word. Given this potential for confusion in the translation process, it is not surprising that interpreter errors have found their way into published reports of Ed's testimony. Sign language is excellent for describing objects, actions, relationships and emotions.

The primary components of English grammar are *word order* and *word suffixes*. But in American Sign Language, word order within a phrase is very flexible. In sign language, one could correctly say *blue car*, as you could say *car blue*.

The primary component in American Sign Language is *space*. The order of phrases within a sentence is strictly regulated. But in English, phrase order is quite flexible.

American Sign Language is a *conceptually linear* language. Events are signed in the exact order in which they take place, quite unlike English, which allows great flexibility in time-sequence structures. For example, when speaking you might say, "I'll stay home if it rains today." Or you could just as easily say, "If it rains today I'll stay home." Only the second phrase pattern is permitted in American Sign Language; conditions always come before conclusions. It works that way in life, and so it works that way in ASL as well.

Another example is the difference in which the two languages structure time. In written and spoken English, the use of prepositions to show time; before, after, and until. For example, "You can start the car after you fasten your seat belt." The English sentence *first* talks about starting the car, *then* it discuss fastening the seat belt. This order of phrasing "contradicts" the intended meaning of the sentence, which would not be allowed in ASL. If you want your audience to first fasten the seat belt, then you must sign that action first. Then you can discuss starting the car. It works that way in life, and so it works that way in American Sign Language.

A problem arises any time Ed Hoffman tells his story in sign language especially in the description of several events happening at the same time. Since American Sign Language's time structure is sequential, expressing simultaneous events becomes much more complicated. Any interpreter who is unfamiliar with the logistics of Dealey Plaza, the adjacent railroad yard, and Stemmons freeway will have interpretation difficulties.

Interpreters unfamiliar with the details of Ed's story often mistranslate plurals for singular. Most nouns in American Sign Language do not have a distinct plural form. "Man" and "men" are signed identically. Ed has never changed his story, but the interpretation of this same story has had a number of interpretations simply because of the interpreter. He sometimes refers to the *police officer* standing by the railroad bridge, and the interpreter has voiced *policemen* for Ed's singular *policeman*.

Sometimes translation errors occur when there is a similarity between a standard sign and an unusual body gesture. For example, Ed described how he wanted to get the attention of the officer on the railroad bridge, but was frightened by the Secret Service agent pointing the rifle. Ed demonstrated how he quickly lowered his arms and the interpreter misunderstood and voiced, "They turned off the light."

Finally, the stress of simultaneous interpretation under less-than-best conditions can cause translation errors. Many years ago, Ed was telling his story to a large group with the aid of a very skilled interpreter. At one point, the interpreter missed a negative marker in one of Ed's signs, so she voiced a sentence which meant the exact opposite of what he said.

The reader should understand the authors are not faulting the interpreters who have made mistakes in the process of simultaneous translation. Through the years, Ed has been accused of "changing his story." Ed has never changed his story, but translation errors have been published without correction.

Sign Language Interpreting

Sign language interpreting makes communication possible between people who are deaf or hard of hearing and people who can hear. Interpreting is a complex process that requires a high degree of linguistic, cognitive and technical skills in both English and American Sign Language. Sign language interpreting, like spoken language interpreting, involves more than simply replacing a word of spoken English with a signed representation of that English word. American Sign Language (ASL) has its own grammatical rules, sentence structure and cultural nuances.

Interpreters must thoroughly understand the subject matter in which they work so that they are able to convert information for one language, known as the "source language" into another, known as the "target language." In addition, interpretations can incorporate cultural information associated with the languages used.

Most sign language interpreters either interpret, which means working between English and ASL, or they transliterate, which is working between spoken English and a form of a signed language that uses a more English-based word order. Some interpreters specialize in oral interpreting for the deaf or hard of hearing who can read lips instead of sign. Other specialties include tactile signing, which is interpreting for persons who are blind as well as deaf by conveying signs directly into a person's hand.

An interpreter's work begins before arriving at the location. The interpreter must become familiar with the subject matter that the speaker will discuss, a task that may involve research on topic-related words and phrases that may be used from both languages. Some interpreters may not specialize in a particular field while many do focus on one area of expertise such as business, law, medicine, or education.

Two Types of Interpretation

There are two methods of interpretation: simultaneous and consecutive. Simultaneous interpretations require the interpreter to listen and sign, or watch and speak, at the same time.

The interpreter begins to convey a sentence in the "target language" while listening or watching the message being delivered in the "source language." This type of interpreting happens most commonly in business meetings and educational settings.

In contrast, consecutive interpretation begins only after the speaker has spoken or signed a sentence or paragraph. Interpreters may need to take notes to assist in the process of creating a coherent and accurate translation. This form of interpretation is used most often for witness testimony in legal settings or in one-on-one meetings such as with a doctor, social worker or counselor. In both simultaneous and consecutive interpreting, the interpreter sits in proximity to the English speaker to allow the deaf person to see the interpreter as well as the facial and body expressions of the English speaker.

Because of the need for a high degree of concentration in both types of interpretation and because of the physical demands of the work, interpreters often work in pairs, with each interpreting 20-to-30 minute segments.

Photo 49: Ed Hoffman attended the Texas School for the Deaf, Austin, Texas

It is the interpreter's primary responsibility to enable deaf or hard of hearing persons the opportunity to communicate freely with hearing individuals. In order to do this, they must be given enough information about a particular assignment to allow time to determine if it's a situation where they can perform professionally. Content may be shared so the interpreter must determine if they have sufficient knowledge or skill to adequately convey the information in both languages. Interpreters strive to remain unbiased toward the content of their work and not alter or modify the meaning or tone of what is conveyed.

In the field of interpreting, as in other professions, appropriate credentials are an important indicator of an interpreter's qualifications. The National Association of the Deaf (NAD) and the National Institute for the Deaf (NID) awards certifications to interpreters who successfully pass its national testing process. These tests consist of interpretation and communication skills, as wells as knowledge, judgment and decision-making skills.

An interpreter holding a national rating of Level V is sufficiently qualified to interpret sign language for any legal proceeding. Unfortunately, the interpreter that was used during the meeting between Ed Hoffman and Jim Marrs was not ASL qualified and a number of key mistakes were made during their conversation. The interpreter hired by Nigel Turner during the filming of Ed's segment for the documentary, "The Men Who Killed Kennedy," was not ASL qualified. He admitted that in an attempt to quickly translate Ed's story he missed some signs and substituted Ed's communication with his own interpretation.

Ed Hoffman's Written English

American Sign Language is Ed's primary language, and English is second. Ed's written English might follow ASL grammatically, and the sentence may appear unintelligible to the non-signer. When FBI agent Will Griffin first met Ed Hoffman in 1977, he classified Ed as "semi-illiterate."

Ed Hoffman has had a profound hearing loss since early childhood. Deaf adults with this same level of hearing loss, age of onset, and language management will, when communication with a hearing non-signer, write a short note of one sentence to *introduce a topic*. Then they elaborate with gestures and crude sketches. More courageous individuals may even try to vocalize key words. Further writing of text may consist of one or two word sentences to explain the meaning of specific gestures, signs, and sketches. They may offer one or two word responses to written questions. It was in this context that Ed attempted to communicate with the FBI in 1967, and again in 1977.

The issue is further complicated by the ease at which a deaf person, who is handling English as a second language, can misunderstand the intent of a written questions put to them by a hearing person. This problem occurs frequently when trying to communicate with deaf people over the telephone via a Telecommunications Device for the Deaf, or TDD.

Ron Friedrich, Ed's minister in Grand Prairie, would often receive faxes or emails from Ed asking Ron to help clarify their meanings. Ed may understand the meaning of individual words, but the meaning he ascribes to them along with the complex grammatical structure, makes it difficult for Ed to fully understand its true significance.

When Ron and Ed would converse via a TDD and the subject matter became complex, they would schedule a face-to-face appointment where they could both "discuss" it using sign language. If they had difficulty in communicating in written English, imagine the problem in communicating with a non-signing person.

No intention is meant to imply that Ed Hoffman is some kind of "Forrest Gump" character. On the contrary, he is an intelligent, alert and sincere individual who is fully aware of complicated issues of politics and finance. It comes down to this, English is a foreign language to Ed Hoffman and he is to be commended for succeeding as well as he does.

In this context, the authors want the reader to analyze the only written statement by Ed Hoffman released by the Federal Bureau of Investigation. This letter, written to Senator Ted Kennedy in 1975, was Ed's attempt to contact someone who could make a difference. The authors suspect that one of the factual errors in the 1977 FBI report where Hoffman is reported as saying, "Both men ran north on the railroad tracks..." may be a simple misreading of this letter. It is also possible Bill Sloan's repeat of this error in his book, "JFK: Breaking the Silence" (1993), may have come either from Ed's letter, the FBI's misreading of this letter, or from interpreter error.

The full text of Ed's letter is shown below. Ed typed the entire text himself using upper case letters. Apply the issue of potential misunderstanding mentioned above to Ed's letter, particularly to the second sentence that summarizes in eight words what he saw on November 22.

OCTOBER 3, 1975,
SEN.TED KENNEDY
WASHINGTON, D.C.

DEAR MR. KENNEDY,

NOW I WISH TO TALK YOU ABOUT YOUR BROTHER'S JOHN F. KENNEDY. SINCE LONG TIMES AGO I REMEMBER WHAT I SAW TWO MEN RAN ON RAILROAD FROM A FENCE. I NEVER TO FORGET A THING IN DALLAS. I WAS SORRY, BECAUSE I AM DEAFNESS TO TALK HARD ABOUT A THING.

I TALKED TO F. B. I'S OFFICE IN DALLAS LAST 1968 OR CAN'T REMEMBER DATE A YEAR AGO.
IF YOU FIND TO SEE F.B.I'S REPORT ABOUT I TALKED THEM.
I GUESS, MAYBE F.B.I. DID NOT UNDERSTAND WHAT I TALKED A THING, BECAUSE I AM DEAFNESS AND HARD TO TALK F.B.I.

BY MY UNCLE AND FATHER TOLD ME BE CAREFUL, BECAUSE IF SOMEON WILL HEAR WHAT I SAY THINGS FROM THE C.I.A OR OTHER PERSONS OR WILL BE VERY DANGEROUS? IF YOU THINK THIS?

IF YOU WILL HELP ME AND TELL SOME THINGS, THANK YOU MUCH.

RESPECTFULLY,

/s/
VIRGIL EDWARD HOFFMAN

Guess Who's Coming
To Dinner?

"One hundred percent reliable. Eddie would never lie about something like that."

LIEUTENANT ROBERT HOFFMAN
DALLAS POLICE DEPARTMENT

Thanksgiving Day, 1963

On Thursday, November 28, just six days after the assassination, the Hoffman family gathered for Thanksgiving dinner at the home of Ed's paternal grandparents. In an effort to stall Ed's persistent requests to call the authorities, Frederick Hoffman promised his son that he would be able to tell his story to his uncle, Robert. At the time of the assassination, Robert Hoffman was a detective with the Dallas police department and was currently assigned to the auto theft unit

When Robert Hoffman arrived, Frederick told Ed to sit and wait while he talked to Robert privately. Ed assumed that his father told his uncle every detail of what had he had seen behind the picket fence.

When Ed was called to join the conversation, he explained the events using sign language to his father. Frederick related his son's signs and gestures for Robert.

When Ed finished telling his story, Robert got up from the chair and spoke to Ed, with Frederick translating. Robert told Frederick to tell Ed, "Your father is right, you should keep quiet about this, and you might be in danger."

Ed protested that the real killers had gotten away and he was confident that the authorities did not know about the shot fired from behind the fence. Ed insisted that someone look into that fact.

Bob responded, with Frederick interpreting, "You keep quiet! You talk, you get shot!" At that point Ed realized that no one was going to help him and he left the room. His father encouraged him to forget what happened, and to enjoy the evening. But he could do neither.

Author Bill Sloan interviewed Robert Hoffman about this Thanksgiving conversation of November 1963. On pages 30-31 of "JFK: Breaking the Silence" (1993), Sloan writes,

> "All I understood was that some people in a car had pointed a gun at Eddie, and his father was concerned about his safety...His father was very, very concerned that Eddie knew anything about the assassination at all..."

Sloan asked Robert Hoffman what he would have advised Ed to do if he had comprehended the full import of his nephew's story.

> "That's difficult to answer...If I had known the whole thing, I guess it would have been my duty to come forward with the information, and I imagine Chief [Jesse Curry] would like to have known about it. But as a relative, I would probably have felt pretty much like Eddie's father — the less said the better..."

Sloan asked Robert if he thought Ed was putting himself in physical danger by making his story public.

> "I don't know, a lot of witnesses obviously did because some of them died. The same could have happened to Eddie."

Robert Hoffman confirmed to Sloan he accurately reported what he had told him about the Thanksgiving conversation. However, there are differences in each person's recollection about that conversation. Several explanations can be made for these differences:

- Both Robert and Ed have a flawed memories of that Thanksgiving conversation.

- After only a few days of discussing Ed's concerns, Frederick still did not yet fully understand that Ed actually may have seen the shot that killed the President. Frederick could tell Robert only as much as he himself understood.

- Frederick understood what Ed saw, but "filtered" his translation to Robert, so that Robert would still not have all of the information.

- Frederick understood what Ed saw, and both Ed and Frederick communicated clearly enough that Robert "got the whole picture." If this were the case, Robert would have found himself in difficult position of having to choose between family loyalty and professional responsibility.

- Had he chosen family over profession, Robert would be understandably reluctant to publicly admit it.

Whichever of these scenarios is correct, the authors find it significant that Robert Hoffman told author Bill Sloan that he considered his nephew to be a truthful and honest person. Robert Hoffman also told Sloan that Ed's father was convinced that his son's life could have been in danger had he gone to the authorities with the information.

On November 26, 2007, the authors conducted a phone interview with Robert Hoffman. The following is a summary of that interview.

At the time of President Kennedy's assassination, Robert Hoffman was a detective assigned to the Dallas police department's auto theft bureau. Hoffman told the authors that on the day of the President's visit, neither he nor anyone in his unit were given any assignments relating to the motorcade or the security of the President. "That was the patrol division's job," Hoffman said.

Robert Hoffman told the authors that only a small percentage of the department's plain clothes officers had assignments related to the President's visit.

According to Hoffman, "It was just another work day, nothing special as far as we were concerned." Even after hearing about the shooting of the President, Hoffman said no one from his squad was asked to assist the investigation.

Regarding the Thanksgiving conversation, the conversation between him and his brother Frederick was very short. He recalled that Frederick was very concerned about his son's safety, but promised Ed that he would be given a chance to tell his story. According to Robert, Ed's father knew sign language and translated what Ed said about the activity of the two men he saw in Dealey Plaza.

Without hesitation, Robert acknowledged that the conversation between himself, Ed, and Frederick did take place. Robert said he watched Ed communicate to his father about seeing men with guns in the parking lot, about seeing the President's wounds and having a weapon pointed at him. Robert told the authors that he believed Ed accurately reported what he had seen and never thought Ed was "telling a wild tale."

Robert Hoffman stated that no one in the family ever questioned Ed's credibility or honesty. Robert told the authors, "I believed his story right away." and "Ed was one hundred percent reliable, he would never lie about something like that."

Robert said during the conversation between Ed, Frederick, and himself, Ed's grandmother was brought into the conversation and they all tried to convince Ed the man he saw with the gun was a Secret Service agent protecting the President. Robert said no matter what they told Ed, he was convinced the man in the business suit shot the President, and this man was *not* Lee Harvey Oswald.

Robert was asked, "Was Ed's father trying to protect Ed?" Robert replied, "Of course he was, lots of people were being killed if they knew anything about this murder."

Leveling the Playing Field

"My son and I were standing there along the curb and I told Joey to wave and then a shot rang out...I thought that someone was shooting from the fence, not the building."

CHARLES BREHM

Visibility from the Freeway

Ed Hoffman has been criticized on 3 primary points regarding his observations of November 22, 1963. Each one deals with the issue of visibility. Ed Hoffman's critics focus on the notion there was some type of vision obstruction between him and the west side of the Texas School Book Depository. Examining the available photographs taken on the day of the assassination, nothing can be found, either natural or man-made, which would have interfered with Hoffman's view.

These same critics of Hoffman concentrate on four specific points regarding Hoffman's observations: (1) a large section of trees on the embankment between his position and the parking lot blocked his view; (2) a large billboard on this same embankment was in his direct line of sight; (3) one witness testified that a train was parked on the tracks over Elm Street at the time of the assassination, thereby blocking his view completely; and, (4) the distance between Hoffman's location and the book depository was too great for Hoffman to see such precise details. Each of these points will be addressed in this chapter.

(1) The Trees

Today, only a small portion of the northeast corner of the book depository can be seen through the trees. The trees along the railroad embankment begin at a point where Elm Street and the triple underpass meet. The trees run parallel along the railroad embankment to the north and end just south of the railroad bridge above Stemmons Freeway.

It is important to remember, on the day of the assassination, there were no trees on the railroad embankment that would have blocked Hoffman's view to the parking lot on the west side of the Book Depository. An aerial photo taken after 1966 (Photo 52) shows there were still no trees along the railroad embankment at that time.

In 1977, when Hoffman contacted the FBI a second time, Special Agent Udo Specht went with Hoffman to Stemmons Freeway and took color photographs of the area. Specht's field report states "...the roadway (Stemmons) is at the same level of the first floor of the Book Depository." How was Specht able to make that determination if trees blocked his view from the highway to the parking lot? The answer was simple — there were no trees in blocking the view.

From his position on Stemmons Freeway, Hoffman had a 360 ° field view of the area. From the available photographs taken the day of the assassination, there were no trees between his elevated position on the freeway to the parking lot on the west side of the book depository or of the triple underpass. The critics who continue to state that Hoffman's view was blocked by a thick growth of trees should re-examine the available photographs taken on November 22, 1963. At the time of the assassination, the trees on the grassy knoll were smaller and were not hanging over the picket fence. On that day, Hoffman had a clear view of the north side of the picket fence.

Photo 50: This Mel McIntire photo, looks east towards the triple underpass from the Elm Street entrance ramp onto Stemmons Freeway. There are no trees along the railroad embankment. The treetops seen in back of the billboard are actually on the south side of the annex road next to the Depository.

Photo 51: This second Mel McIntire photo shows more of the railroad embankment to the north. The arrow points to a leafless bush in the open area which is between the embankment and Stemmons Freeway. This bush was not in Hoffman's line of sight.

Northbound Stemmons Freeway

Ed Hoffman

Photo 52: This photo taken after 1966, looks east towards the book depository. When this photo was taken, there were no visual obstructions between Hoffman's location and the picket fence.

The circle around to the almost leafless bush seen also in Photo 51.

Picket fence

Photo 53: This 2007 photo, taken from the backside of the billboard, looks east towards the book depository. A thick growth of overhanging trees now blocks much of the north side of the picket fence from view.

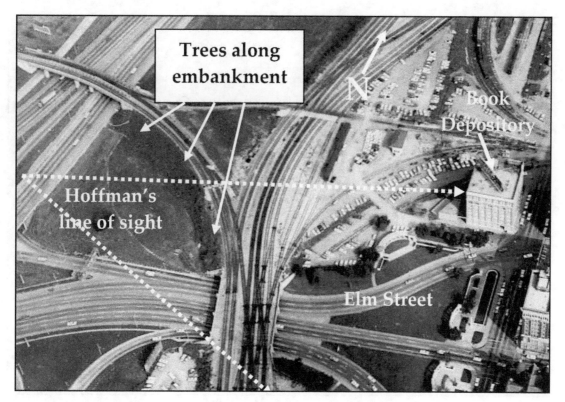

Photo 54: This undated photo now shows a line of trees along the railroad embankment. It is not known when this row of trees was planted at this location.

Photo 55: This is a close-up of Photo 54. When this photo was taken, the billboard's location and angle to Elm Street had not been changed.

Photo 56: This photo, taken from the west side of the triple underpass was part of the Secret Service's investigation in 1963. This view looks west towards Stemmons Freeway. The arrow points to Hoffman's location on Stemmons Freeway. Note there are no trees yet planted along this route as seen in Photos 58 and 57.

Photo 57: This photo was taken by the authors in August of 2007. Ed Hoffman stood at this location on the west side of the northbound lanes of Stemmons Freeway on the day of the assassination. When this photograph was taken, the trees along the railroad embankment, east of the freeway, nearly block the view of the Texas School Book Depository.

Photo 58: In this undated photo, the trees between the railroad bridge and the billboard are as tall as the embankment (circle) and additional plantings have been added to the area. This view looks northwest over Stemmons Freeway.

Photo 59: This close-up of Photo 58 shows the single row of trees along Elm Street between the underpass and Stemmons Freeway.

(2) THE BILLBOARD

On November 22, 1963, a large billboard faced motorists as they traveled east along Main and Commerce streets and into Dealey Plaza. Motorists traveling west on Elm from Dealey Plaza towards Stemmons Freeway would have seen it in their rearview mirrors. The distance from Hoffman's location on the west side of Stemmons Freeway to this billboard is 164 yards.

On the day of the assassination, the advertisement displayed on the billboard was for Old Charter bourbon. The advertisement was mounted on the steel frame of the structure with the bottom edge of the sign about 3 feet above the ground. The following photos show the positioning the billboard and viewing access of Ed Hoffman.

Photo 60: This photo was taken by the Secret Service and used in their investigation of the assassination. The Old Charter billboard is seen at the left margin of the photo.

Photo 61: This is a cropped version of Photo 60 showing the height of the sign.

Photo 62: This view of the billboard was taken from a point 100 yards west of the triple underpass. The dashed line in this photo represents the height of the billboard in relation to the triple overpass as it appeared in 2007. The top of the Old Charter billboard would have been was just above the black line.

Photo 63: This previously unpublished photo shows the height of the billboard compared to the top of the triple underpass. This photo was taken from the back window of a car traveling west on Main Street. The photo's horizon line has been corrected for the comparison.

Photo 64: This photo was taken after 1966. The solid line represents the angle of the billboard compared to Elm Street (black dashed line). The angle of the billboard is about 65 degrees off of Elm Street. The location and angle of the sign had not been changed when this photo was taken.

Photo 65: This photo of the back of the billboard shows the additional steel I-beam which was added to the billboard's original frame. From the arrow to the ground is 16 feet.

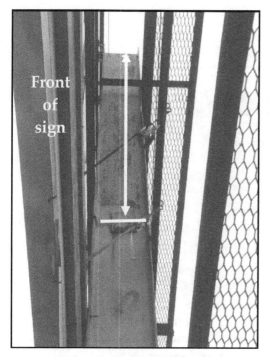

Photo 66: The white line is the connecting point between the 2 steel I-beams. The top I-beam is fourteen feet in length.

Photo 67: This is a close-up of the steel plate that joins the two I-beams on the backside of the billboard.

Photo 68: This view looks northeast towards the triple underpass from the south curb of Commerce Street. The dashed line shows the height of the billboard as it appeared in August 2007 in relation to the top of the triple underpass.

Photo 69: Looking west towards Stemmons Freeway from the west end of the parking lot behind the Book Depository. The arrow points to Ed's position on Stemmons (behind here the billboard is now). Only a small portion of Stemmons Freeway can be seen in this photo (circle).

Photo 70: This undated photo was taken from on top of the triple underpass looking west along Elm Street towards Stemmons Freeway. The solid white line on the back of the billboard represents the height as it was on the day of the assassination.

Photo 71: The dashed lines represent the dimensions of the original Old Charter billboard which have been superimposed on the current billboard.

switchbox

Photo 72: This photo was taken from the east edge of the picket fence looking west towards the back of the billboard. The arrow points to Ed Hoffman's location on Stemmons Freeway. The rear side of the billboard is outlined with the white line. The middle switchbox (now removed) has been added to the photo as a point of reference.

(3) A Train on the Triple Underpass

Ed Hoffman has maintained he saw a slow-moving freight train move from south to north over the top of the triple underpass moments after the shooting. Hoffman has claimed he saw a uniformed Dallas police officer cross from the west side to the east side of the triple underpass just as the train passed the officer's position. This took place just after Hoffman saw the President's limousine pass beneath his elevated position on Stemmons Freeway

Hoffman's critics are quick to dismiss his statement about a passing train based solely on the available photographs taken just before and immediately after the assassination. However, the two Dallas police officers who were assigned to the triple underpass mentioned a passing train during their interviews with the FBI, but only one officer mentioned it during their appearance before the Warren Commission. In addition, one of these officers told a researcher a three engine locomotive passed by as the motorcade approached the triple underpass.

In an attempt to reach a definitive conclusion regarding the train issue, the authors examined those witnesses who made reference to a train in either a sworn affidavit, during an FBI interview or in testimony before the Warren Commission. The majority of the witnesses examined here were not asked nor did they volunteer any information about seeing a train on top of the triple underpass. This may be due to the fact a moving train was not viewed as relevant to the investigation of the shooting of President Kennedy. As a result, only 3 witnesses who testified before the Warren Commission were asked about a train. Those witnesses who did make statements about a train will be examined in the next section.

Dallas Police and the Triple Underpass

At 10 a.m. on November 18, 1963 — four days before the assassination — Secret Service agents Winston Lawson and Forrest Sorrels met with Dallas police Deputy Chief Lunday and Assistant Chief Batchelor to finalize the manpower requirements for the presidential motorcade. On page 3 of Commission Document 81, Batchelor writes,

> …have men on each railroad and traffic overpass that the presidential party would go under, and that these people should be instructed not to let anyone stand over the immediate path of the presidential party…they want from two to four men assigned at each of these points.

One of the two uniformed police officers assigned to the triple underpass during the motorcade was James W. Foster. His primary duty while on top of the triple underpass was to prevent anyone from standing directly over the Presidential motorcade as it moved through Dealey Plaza.

Officer James C. White was the other uniformed police officer assigned to the top of the triple underpass on November 22, 1963. White and Foster both worked in the traffic division and their direct supervisor was Sergeant D. V. Harkness.

Regardless of who gave Foster and White the assignment on the triple underpass, logic would suggest the directives from the Secret Service regarding security would have been passed on to the officers assigned to areas in close proximity to the President. Were the Secret Service directives given to the officers who were assigned to the other overpasses along the motorcade route? We can only assume they were.

Officer Foster

On December 4, 1963, Officer Foster submitted a typed one-page report describing his actions and observations on November 22, 1963. This report was addressed to Jesse Curry, Chief of Police who forwarded the report to the Warren Commission. Foster's report was labeled Commission Exhibit 1358 and can be found in Volume 22 on page 605. Foster's report states he was given his assignment on top of the triple underpass by Lieutenant Southard. However, in this Warren Commission testimony on April 9, 1964, he claims his immediate supervisor, Sergeant D. V. Harkness had assigned him and Officer J. C. White to this post.

Officer J. W. Foster was interviewed by FBI Special Agent E.J. Robertson on March 25, 1964. Agent Robertson writes,

> FOSTER stated he arrived at this station at approximately 10:15 AM on this date and immediately took up a point on the railroad overpass overlooking the triple intersection. He stated that his instructions were not to permit anyone on the overpass.

> Patrolman FOSTER stated that he did not permit anyone on the overpass except about nine Union Terminal railroad employees that appeared to be working in the area and moved to the east edge of the overpass shortly prior to the arrival of the Presidential motorcade.

On April 9, 1964, Officer Foster appeared before Warren Commission counsel Joseph Ball in the United States Attorney's office in Dallas. During his testimony, Officer Foster was directed to make a sketch of Dealey Plaza and to indicate where he was standing at the time of the assassination.

> **Ball:** Now, where were you standing?
> **Foster:** Standing along the east curb of — east side of the overpass over Elm Street there. About the south curb.
> **Ball:** Over, above the south curb of Elm?
> **Foster:** Yes, sir.
> **Ball:** Will you put a mark on there? Mark an "X" where you were standing and write your initials right next to that "X. What are your initials?
> **Foster:** J.W.
> **Ball:** J.W. F. That marks where you were standing?
> **Foster:** Approximately; yes, sir.
> (Volume 6, pgs 247-253)

During his testimony, Foster answered in the affirmative that he didn't quite fulfill his responsibilities to the best of his ability. Rather than ask Officer Foster if he had any specific

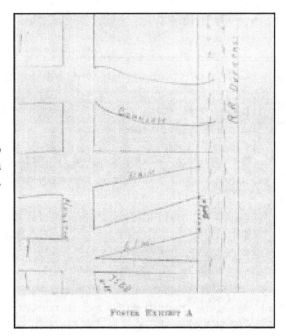

Photo 73: This sketch was entered into evidence as Foster Exhibit A and is in Volume 19 on page 769.

Photo 74: This aerial view of the triple underpass shows the positions of Officers Foster and White during the assassination. The dashed line represents the southbound train as described by both officers.

instructions regarding who could be on the overpass, Ball told Foster what his instructions were by way of a leading question,

> **Ball:** Now you had instructions to keep all unauthorized personnel off of that overpass?
> **Foster:** Yes, sir.
> **Ball:** Did you do that?
> **Foster:** Yes, sir.
> **Ball:** Did you permit some people to be there?
> **Foster:** Yes, sir.
> **Ball:** Who?
> **Foster:** People that were working for the railroad there.
> **Ball:** Were there many people?
> **Foster:** About 10 or 11.

Rather than have Foster explain why he allowed railroad employees to be on the overpass, Mr. Ball moved onto a different topic. Not only did Officer Foster fail to follow the orders of his supervisor, he chose to ignore the directives of the United States Secret Service.

During this exchange, Mr. Ball's use of the word "unauthorized" is problematic. Which railroad worker qualified as "authorized?" Who would be considered an unauthorized person? Before being dismissed, Counsel Ball asked the witness a valid question,

> **Ball:** You did permit some railroad employees to remain on the overpass?
> **Foster:** Yes, sir.
> **Ball:** How did you determine they were railroad employees?
> **Foster:** By identification they had with them. Identification they had and the other men that was with them verifying that they were employees.
> **Ball:** Okay.
> (Volume 6, p. 252).

Officer Foster and the Train

In his report to Chief Curry, Foster said he was standing against the east railing of the triple underpass as the motorcade passed underneath. He does not mention a passing train while on top of the overpass.

On March 25, 1964, Foster was interviewed by FBI agent E. J. Robertson and in that report he tells Robertson "… a freight train passed moving in a southerly direction." Foster told Agent Robertson as the train moved from north to south, it blocked his view of the east side of the overpass.

Foster's location is marked on photo 74. What is puzzling is how a train passing behind Foster could block his view of the motorcade passing in front of him. Unfortunately, that question was not asked.

On April 8, 1964, when Foster appeared before the Warren Commission, he was not asked about nor did he volunteer any information about a passing train.

When interviewed for "No More Silence," Officer Foster admitted a train did pass by while he was on the overpass. Sneed writes,

At the time the motorcade came through, there were about seven or eight people up there…just prior to the shots, a three engine locomotive went by, so there wasn't a lot that you could see or hear from up there even though the locomotive had already passed and just the boxcars were going by at the time the motorcade passed through. (Page 212).

Officer Foster and Larry Sneed

Assassination researcher Larry Sneed interviewed Officer Foster for his book "No More Silence" (1998). On page 211, Sneed writes,

Our orders were to keep all personnel off the railroad overpass. During the morning, there were several people who came up, and I told them they had to leave. I checked the ID's of the railroad people and tried to get them to leave, but they had the idea that I couldn't do that.

If I'd have gotten them off, they would have probably pulled the engine up right behind me, which would have created a noise problem. So there wasn't much I could do about it.

During this interview with Sneed, Foster could have been asked about the identification these "railroad people" showed, which engine would they have pulled up right behind him, and was there an engine already on the tracks when he arrived at his post? Unfortunately, these questions were not asked.

There was a simple solution to this problem of moving people off the top of the underpass — order them to leave and if they refuse, place them under arrest and physically remove them. Had Foster exercised his authority, this breach of security could have been avoided.

Everything Officer Foster did that day with regards to his responsibilities while on the triple underpass rings of incompetence and negligence. Foster was not reprimanded by his immediate supervisor, or asked to explain his actions to the United States Secret Service.

Officer Foster and Sam Holland

The testimony of another eyewitness to the activities of Officer Foster should be noted here. Sam Holland, signal supervisor for the Union Terminal Railroad, stood on the triple underpass during the assassination along with about 15 other railroad employees. Why they were allowed to remain on the overpass, directly over the top of the motorcade, remains a mystery.

Holland appeared before the Commission on April 8, 1964, one day before Officer Foster gave his testimony. Warren Commission counsel Samuel Stern asked Holland to describe what he did in regards to the assassination. Holland testified,

Well, about 11:00 o'clock a couple of policemen and a plainclothesman, came up on top of the triple underpass, and we had some men working up there…and I

Photo 75: Assassination eyewitness Sam Holland stands on top of the triple underpass in the same spot where he stood on the November 22, 1963. The dashed line outlines the south edge of the picket fence on the grassy knoll. When this photo was taken, the trees did not block the view of the fence from the underpass.

left my office and walked up to the underpass to talk to the policemen. And they asked me during the parade if I would come back up there and identify people that was supposed to be on the overpass. That is, railroad people. (Volume 6, page 239)

Later in Holland's testimony he was asked about the two police officers who were stationed on the triple underpass:

Stern: And these policemen that you spoke to, there were 3 altogether?
Holland: Two — there were 2 city policemen and 1 man in plainclothes. I didn't talk to him. I talked to the city policemen.
Stern: You don't know what his affiliation was?
Holland: I know he was a plainclothes detective, or FBI agent or something.
(Volume 6, p. 239)

Approximately two-and-one-half pages of Holland's testimony consists of Stern trying to get Holland to provide the names of the other railroad workers who were on top of the triple underpass on the day of the assassination. To fully appreciate the exchange between Stern and Holland, the reader is encouraged to read Sam Holland's entire testimony in Volume 6, pages 239-248.

On page 241, the following exchange between Mr. Stern and Holland can best be described as unusual,

> **Holland:** Now, like I said a while ago, by the time they started there was quite a few come up there, but I can't remember who it was or their names, because...
> **Stern:** Before the motorcade started?
> **Holland:** Before the motorcade started.
> **Stern:** These were people you recognized as employees?
> **Holland:** Some of them, and some of them I did not recognize, but I think he was asking for credentials.
> **Stern:** The uniformed policeman?
> **Holland:** Yes; one on that side, and one on this side to keep them...
> **Stern:** Yes; and did you participate in identifying people as being terminal or railroad employees?
> **Holland:** When they first started arriving, yes; it was my purpose for going up there.
> **Stern:** So, that it is fair to say that at the time the President's motorcade turned into this area, there was no one on the overpass that you didn't know either as Terminal Co. employees, or railroad employees, or as a policeman?
> **Holland:** Wouldn't be fair to say that, because there was quite a few come up there right in the last moments.
> **Stern:** There were? Tell us about that.
> **Holland:** That I couldn't recognize. There wasn't too many people up there, but there were a few that came up there the last few minutes, but the policemen were questioning them and getting their identification, and, (Holland's statement was cut off in mid-sentence by Stern).

Apparently Officer Foster, on his own, decided to ignore the directives of his supervisor and the Secret Service by allowing railroad workers to remain on top of the triple underpass. In addition, these workers, who he did not know, were allowed to stand directly over the top of the President as he passed directly below them in an open car. According to Sam Holland, there were some "railroad workers" even he did not recognize, but yet Officer Foster allowed them to stay on the overpass.

According to Sam Holland, there were some people on the overpass, that even he did not recognize, but yet they were allowed to stay there in direct conflict with the directives of the Secret Service. This is another example of Officer Foster's inability to follow orders.

Officer Foster and James Altgens

Another eyewitness who dealt with Officer Foster on top of the triple underpass was United Press photographer, James "Ike" Altgens. Altgens walked onto the overpass at about 11:15 a.m., looking for a good spot to take photographs. Altgens testified,

> ...When I arrived on the triple underpass there was no one up there but two uniformed policemen and one of the uniformed policemen came over to me

and asked me if I was a railroad employee and I told him "no," and I showed him my press tag and told him I had a Department of Public Safety ID card showing I was connected with the AP...the policeman said, "Well I'm sorry, but this is private property. It belongs to the railroad and only railroad employees are permitted on this property.
(Volume 7, pgs 515-525)

Altgens testified the officer [Foster] did not deny him access to the overpass for security reasons but told him it was private property and he was not allowed to stay there. Would it matter if it was private or public property? It did not matter to the Secret Service if the officers assigned to the overpasses were on private property or public property. Their orders were stated simply and directly, "...not to let anyone stand over the immediate path of the presidential party."

Did Foster assume if he allowed only 'authorized" people to remain on the overpass, the Secret Service would consider it permissible? The Secret Service gave their orders to the Assistant Chief of Police believing those orders would be passed on to the officers involved with motorcade security. Logic would suggest the Secret Service naturally expected the orders would be followed without question. Apparently some officers made their own decisions regarding security.

Wouldn't Foster's supervisor have passed along the orders of the Secret Service when he assigned Foster to the triple underpass? The directive of keeping people off the overpass would include "authorized" and "unauthorized."

Officer White

Dallas Officer James C. White states he was assigned on top of the triple underpass on the west side, and his responsibility was to keep people off of the overpass while the motorcade passed through the area. On December 4, 1963, Officer White submitted a one page report to Chief Curry regarding his activities on the day of the assassination. In the second paragraph of this report White wrote,

A Texas and Pacific freight train was traveling North on the railroad tracks between the parade and me... as soon as the train cleared the tracks, to where I could cross to where the search was being made, I went to the location to help block off the building. (Commission Exhibit 1358, Volume 22, p. 604).

On March 25, 1964, Officer White was interviewed by FBI Special Agent E. J. Robertson. In Robertson's field report, he writes,

...[White] was assigned to a station on the triple railroad overpass at Elm, Main and Commerce Streets for coverage of the motorcade route taken by President KENNEDY... and just prior to the arrival of the motorcade and President KENNEDY, a freight train passed moving in a southerly direction and blocked his view of the east side of the overpass.

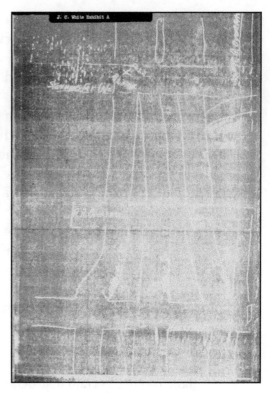

Photo 76: This is a copy of Murphy Exhibit A which was given to Officer White during his testimony. White was instructed to place a circle and his initials indicating where he stood on the triple overpass during the shooting. This exhibit was then remarked White Exhibit A and appears in Volume 21, on page 728.

One sentence in Robertson's report of White is nearly identical to a sentence in the report he filed on Officer Foster. Robertson interviewed both officers on March 25, 1964. In his report on Foster, he wrote, "…a freight train passed headed in a southerly direction." Robertson's report on White states, "…a freight train passed moving in a southerly direction…"

Other verbiage might be more common when describing this event, for example, "A southbound train passed through" or "A train moved south along the overpass." Did both officers actually use the words "southerly direction?" Did Robertson insert his own words in both reports or did someone else?

According to FBI's standard procedure regarding their field reports, agents give their field notes to a clerk who then types the formal report using only those notes. Once the report is filed, the original notes are destroyed. It is possible whoever typed the Foster and White reports used their own choice of words to describe the train's direction.

Officer White told agent Robertson a train moved over the triple underpass, but it was just "prior to the arrival of the motorcade." Officer White was not asked when the train passed; before, during, or after the motorcade. The FBI report does not indicate if that question was asked.

It is interesting to note that none of the railroad employees standing on top of the triple underpass mentioned a passing train when they gave statements to the authorities, or during their interviews with the FBI. Were these witnesses ever asked about a passing train? Did the investigators consider a passing train a "non-issue" since it probably was not involved in the assassination of the President?

The FBI report has White stating a train moved north over the triple underpass. Ed Hoffman has communicated he observed a train moving north across the triple underpass as well. Hoffman's train blocked his view of the parking lot on the west side of the book depository. Could officers Foster and White have been confused on which direction they were facing?

Did Hoffman know north from south? Ed has communicated to the authors he knew which direction he was facing and which direction the train was moving. At this point the direction of the train is less important than the fact that Hoffman, White, and Foster, each recall a train passed over the top of the triple underpass shortly before, or moments after the motorcade passed through Dealey Plaza.

On April 9, 1964, Officer White appeared before Warren Commission Assistant Counsel Joseph Ball. White began his testimony at 11:45 a.m., an hour and fifteen minutes after Foster testified. White told Ball he was assigned to the west side of the triple underpass and Officer Foster was stationed on the east side. White described his post as "approximately at the north curb of Main" (Volume 6, pgs 253-256). This would put Officer White slightly south and west of Foster's position on the triple underpass. The triple underpass is 115 feet wide.

Officer White testified,

> **Ball:** You had certain instructions, didn't you?
> **White:** Yes, sir.
> **Ball:** What were they?
> **White:** Not to let any unauthorized personnel on top of the overpass.
> **Ball:** Now, you did permit some people to stay on the overpass, didn't you?
> **White:** Yes, sir.
> **Ball:** Who were they?
> **White:** Workers of the railroad company.
> **Ball:** Were they people you knew?
> **White:** No, sir.
> **Ball:** Well, how did you know they were workers with the railroad company?
> **White:** Majority of them were there when we got there, working on the rails.

Note that it was Officer White and not Mr. Ball who first used the phrase "unauthorized personnel." Why wasn't White asked to clarify the term "unauthorized personnel?" Foster and White violated the directives of the Secret Service by allowing civilians to remain on the overpass and this issue was not resolved by the Warren Commission.

White testified he did not see the President's motorcade on Elm Street,

> **Ball:** Did you see the President come into sight?
> **White:** No, sir; first time I saw it, it had passed under the triple underpass.
> **Ball:** You were too far away to see it, were you?
> **White:** There was a freight train traveling. There was a train passing between the location I was standing and the area from which the procession was traveling, and — a big long freight train, and I did not see it.
> **Ball:** You didn't see the procession?
> **White:** No, sir.

Officer White testified he did not see the President approaching because of a freight train passing between him and Foster at that moment. If this is correct, the train should be visible in the photographs taken by James Altgens and Mel McIntire.

Officer White could have been asked which direction was the train traveling; how many cars were in the train; was the train moving slow or fast as it passed your location; did any other trains pass by during this same time? Unfortunately, Officer White was not asked to clarify his answers about the passing train.

Did the Commission know the Secret Service had instructed the police department to contact the railroads and temporarily suspend the movement of trains until the President's motorcade had passed through the area? This would have been a good question for the Dallas Chief of Police, but the Chief was never asked that question.

Later during his testimony, Mr. Ball asks if he heard anything while he was stationed on the overpass.

> **Ball:** Did you hear any shots?
> **White:** No, sir.
> **Ball:** Didn't?
> **White:** No, sir.
> **Ball:** All right now, you heard no sound of rifle fire or anything?
> **White:** No, sir.
> **Ball:** Freight train was going through at the time?
> **White:** Yes, sir.
> **Ball:** Making noise.
> **White:** Yes, sir; noisy train.

Officer White told FBI Agent Robertson on March 24, 1964:

> He advised that at the time the President was shot, he heard a noise which was possibly the shots fired which killed President KENNEDY, but at the time he thought this noise was caused by torpedo's used by the railroad in directing the movement of freight cars.

During his appearance before the Warren Commission, Officer White denied hearing rifle shots and failed to mention anything about "railroad torpedos."

Officer White's statement to the FBI on March 24, 1964, is a contradiction of his April 9, 1964 Warren Commission testimony. During his interview with the FBI, he believed the "noise" he heard during the assassination was a railroad torpedo. While testifying to the Warren Commission, he denied hearing any shots.

Officer White was not asked if he heard any other noises that sounded like gunshots. It would have been important to know if he heard any noises that sounded like a railroad torpedo or how he could he tell the difference between a gunshot and a railroad torpedo. Sadly, these questions were not asked.

Known by railroad workers simply as a torpedo, this small explosive device attaches to the top of the track. As the wheels of the train come in contact with the device, a small explosive charge is detonated. The explosion can be heard over the noise of the engine, signaling the engineer to reduce speed or stop immediately.

The issue is not if a train moved across the top of the triple underpass, but more importantly, *when* did the train move. This subject is still open for debate. Neither the FBI nor the Warren Commission asked the when question. Asking the "who, what, where, when, and how" questions is the starting point in any investigation.

During his appearance before the Commission, this exchange between Ball and White took place.

> **Ball:** I'm going to get another copy of this map. Let me see, I can use this. Mark this as Exhibit A to your deposition. Now, a diagram that was drawn by a patrolman, Joe Murphy, and he has made some marks and other witnesses have, but don't pay any attention to that. I want you to look at this drawing and take a pen and mark your position on the railroad overpass in a circle, and put your initials beside it. You have made an "X."
> **White:** Yes, sir.
> **Ball:** And you have initialed J. C. White, is that right?
> **White:** Yes, sir.

After making his mark on this poor copy of Murphy Exhibit A, this sketch became White Exhibit A and was entered into the official record. This "new from old" document can be found in Volume 21 on page 728.

Officer Joe Murphy

Officer Joe Murphy was assigned to a post at "Stemmons Freeway Service Rd. OVERPASS (atop overpass), as stated on page 5 of Lawrence Exhibit 2, in Volume 20, pgs. 489-495." Murphy testified to Warren Commission counsel Joseph Ball on April 8, 1964, the day before Officer Foster and White testified. At some point during his testimony, Murphy was asked to draw a sketch of Dealey Plaza. There is nothing in the written transcripts of his testimony instructing him to make such a sketch, as would have been a normal legal proceeding. The first reference to this sketch is when Mr. Ball states,

> **Ball:** Now, you have a map here which you have drawn for us to show your position, is that right?
> (Reporter marked instrument—Murphy Exhibit A, for identification)
> **Murphy:** Yes, that's right.
> **Ball:** And you have drawn a position there as to where you were standing, is that right?
> **Murphy:** That's right.
> **Ball:** All right. Mark the place where you were standing as Position 1, using an "X."
> **Murphy:** All right. (Witness Murphy marked the diagram as requested by Counsel Ball)

Murphy tells Ball he was assigned to a 3-wheeled motorcycle on northbound Stemmons Freeway over the top of Elm Street, and states he was with 2 other motorcycle officers, but could not remember their names. Murphy said from his position on Stemmons,

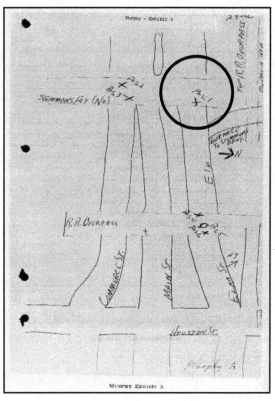

Photo 77: Murphy Exhibit A from Volume 20, page 638. The circle marks Murphy's position on Stemmons Freeway.

Note that Murphy incorrectly drew the entrance ramp on the east side of Stemmons rather than on the west side.

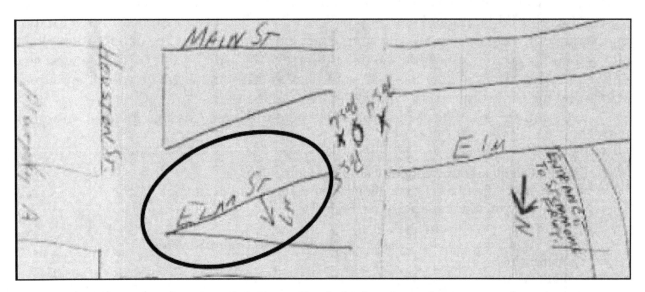

Photo 78: This is a cropped portion of photo 77. The circle shows Murphy's arrow and number "7." Murphy marked this document with an arrow and the number "7" indicating the direction he saw people running after the shooting in Dealey Plaza.

he could see 2 uniformed officers on each side of the triple underpass and 8 to 10 other people. Later in the proceedings, Mr. Ball asks Murphy,

> **Ball:** You heard shots, did you?
> **Murphy:** Yes, I did (says the shots sounded like they came from the east).
> **Ball:** And were there echoes?
> **Murphy:** Yes, quite a few.
> **Ball:** Will you put an arrow showing the direction the people were running and mark that arrow "7" — that's the direction you saw people running?
> **Murphy:** Yes, they were running up in this direction and then in behind this Book Depository.

Officer Brown and the Train

On the day of the assassination, two Dallas police officers were assigned to the railroad bridge over the top of Stemmons Freeway. Officers J. Lomax and E. Brown took up positions on the catwalks on each side of this bridge. Brown testified he and officer Lomax stood on the catwalks on either side of the railroad bridge, with Brown taking a position on the south side of the bridge (Brown refers to this bridge over Stemmons as the "T & P Railroad Overpass").

Recall Hoffman saw a uniformed police officer on the railroad bridge after parking his car on the shoulder of Stemmons Freeway. As Hoffman stood/sat along the west side of the freeway, he watched this officer walking back and forth along this railroad bridge. After the President's limousine passed Hoffman's location, Ed ran along the shoulder of the freeway and tried to get this officers attention. This officer was very likely Earle Brown.

How did Ed Hoffman know any police officers had been assigned to this location on the day of the assassination? The simple fact is Hoffman had to be at a location which allowed him to see this officer on the railroad bridge and still be able to see the west side of the book depository — that location would have been somewhere between the railroad bridge and the triple underpass.

On April 8, 1964, Officer Brown testified before Warren Commission counsel Joseph Ball.

> **Ball:** Did you see any people over in the railroad yards?
> **Brown:** Not that I recall; now they were moving trains in and out.
> **Ball:** But you didn't see people standing?
> **Brown:** No sir; sure didn't.
> **Ball:** Was there any obstruction of your vision to the railroad yards?
> **Brown:** Yes.
> **Ball:** What?
> **Brown:** Not the direction of the railroad yard, but at ground level we didn't have very good view. Mr. Lomax and I remarked that we didn't have a very good view.
> **Ball:** Was that because of the moving trains?
> **Brown:** Yes, sir.

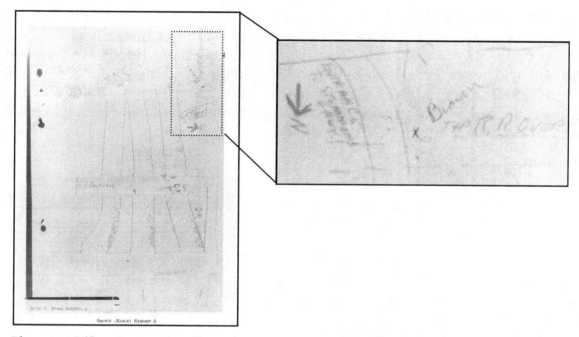

Photo 79: Officer Brown placed an "x" and wrote his name, "Brown" on this sketch of Dealey Plaza. At the time of the assassination, Brown was assigned to the railroad bridge over Stemmons Freeway. This original sketch was drawn by Officer Joe Murphy. After Brown made his mark on this document, the Warren Commission renamed it Brown Exhibit A.

Photo 80: This aerial view of Dealey Plaza shows Officer Brown's location on the railroad bridge as on the day of the assassination.

What did Officer Brown mean when he confirmed "trains were moving in and out." From his statement we can assume at least one train was moving within his field of view while he was on the railroad bridge. Several follow-up questions could have been asked at this point: Did he see more than one train moving in the switching yard; Were these trains moving before or after he heard gunshots; Which direction were these trains moving; Did any trains move across the triple underpass; and were these passenger or freight trains?

Later during his testimony, Brown told Ball,

> **Brown:** ...and then I heard these shots and then I smelled gun powder.
> **Ball:** You did?
> **Brown:** It come on, it would be maybe a couple minutes later so—at least it smelled like it to me. (Volume 6, 231-236)

It is puzzling how Brown was able to smell gunpowder "a couple minutes later" if all the shots fired at President Kennedy came from the 6th floor of the book depository, over 300 yards to the east. How long did he remain at this location before moving into the parking lot? Is it possible that the odor of gunpowder came from another location close by — perhaps from a spot at ground level?

Lee Bowers and the Train

Lee Bowers, a Union Railroad employee, was stationed inside the Union Terminal Company's switching tower on November 22, 1963. From inside the 14-foot tower, Bowers could see the north side of the picket fence, the triple underpass, and the parking lot on the west side of the Texas School Book Depository. Bowers told the Warren Commission that he, "Sealed off the area, and I held off the trains until they could be examined, and there was some transients taken on at least one train."(Volume 6, pgs 284-289). A good follow-up question could have been: "Was a train moving through the switching yard when he held off the trains?"

Unfortunately, this was Bower's last statement and he was dismissed before another question was asked. Regrettably, Mr. Bowers died two years later and we will never know what he meant by "...held off the trains." However, Bowers was able to tell the Warren Commission that this took place a "maximum of 5 minutes" after the shooting. For a more detailed account of Lee Bowers' statement, see chapter 10, *Another Brick in the Wall*.

The Mark Bell film and the Train

A search of photographs and available motion picture films which showed Dealey Plaza before, during and after the shooting, were examined in an attempt to locate a passing freight train as claimed by Hoffman, Foster, and White.

Photographic corroboration for Ed Hoffman's claim regarding a northbound train can be found within several frames of the Mark Bell film. Bell stood on the concrete pillar peristyle at the corner of Main and Houston (Photo 83).

As President Kennedy's limousine turned onto Houston Street, Bell recorded about 15 seconds of the scene, and filmed the presidential limousine as it turned onto Elm Street.

Bell exposed about 60 frames with his movie camera until his view was blocked by the trees on the south side of Elm.

In "Pictures of the Pain" (1994), Richard Trask interviewed Bell who recalled when the President's car began turning from Houston onto Elm Street, Bell jumped down from his elevated position and ran south along Main Street hoping to see the limousine again before it went under the triple underpass. Bell said, "That's when the shots were fired, while I was down, probably no more than 5-10 seconds." Immediately after the last shot, Bell started filming again, and his next sequence recorded the activity in the Plaza in three separate sections (P. 264).

In this second sequence, Bell's camera recorded Dallas motorcycle officer Robert Hargis crossing Elm Street from north to south. Immediately after Hargis crosses Elm, several vehicles carrying members of the press come into the frame from the right. Several citizens can be seen running towards the grassy knoll towards the picket fence.

Dallas motorcycle officer Clyde Haygood can be seen parking his motorcycle against the north curb of Elm, and Mr. Arthur Chism can be seen running west on the sidewalk behind Haygood's position.

While pointing his camera in the direction of the railroad yard, three boxcars of a freight train can be seen in the background. The last three boxcars of this train are about to cross the railroad bridge over Stemmons Freeway. The train has already passed under the signaling tower and has moved out of the switching yard. Because only a few seconds of this sequence was captured on film, it cannot be determined if this train is still moving or has stopped. Regardless, in order for this train to be at this location, it must have crossed the triple underpass from south to north, just as Hoffman claimed.

Judging from the activity recorded on Bell's film, less than 30 seconds has passed since the shooting stopped. When this single frame of Bell's film was exposed, 3 boxcars are approaching the railroad bridge which crosses over Stemmons Freeway. This train is heading west from the switching yard on the north set of tracks. Dallas police officers E. Brown and J. Lomax were assigned to the railroad bridge and this freight train was headed in their direction (Photo 84).

As Photos 81 and 82 clearly show, this train was on one of the two main lines, and since no engine can be seen, we have to assume that at least one engine was pulling these boxcars out of the yard when Bell recorded it on his film. In order for a westbound train to have been on the railroad bridge when it was recorded on Bell's film, it had to cross the triple underpass from south to north, just as Ed Hoffman claims.

Photo 83 depicts Mark Bell's position in Dealey Plaza at the time he filmed the motorcade as it traveled west on Elm Street. From his position, he was able to see over the picket fence and his film recorded the train as it moved across the railroad bridge.

The fact that at least one set of boxcars can be seen on the outbound tracks supports Hoffman's statement that a freight train moved from south to north on the day of the assassination.

Photo 84 was taken by the authors while standing in the middle of the railroad bridge which crosses over the top of Stemmons Freeway. This view looks east towards the Book Depository. From this position to the west side of the Book Depository is approximately 300 yards. The freight train recorded on Mark Bell's film was traveling west on the track to the left in this photo.

Photo 81: This frame from the Mark Bell film shows 3 boxcars on the outbound tracks about to cross over the Stemmons Freeway railroad bridge.

Photo 82: This is a close-up of Photo 85. The arrows points to the last 3 boxcars of an outbound freight train.

Photo 83: The black dot marks the position of the freight train as seen in photo 85. The white dot represents Bell's position in Dealey Plaza. The arrow indicates the direction Mark Bell pointed his camera after the shooting.

Photo 84: This photo from the railroad bridge looks east towards the book depository (black arrow). The white arrow points to the steel divider between the two tracks. Both sets of tracks cross over the top of Stemmons Freeway. Officers Brown and Lomax were assigned to the catwalks on the north and south sides of this railroad bridge.

Photo 85: This aerial photo shows the two sets of tracks that cross over the top of Stemmons Freeway. These tracks are separated by a steel divider that prevents passing trains from striking each other as they move across the bridge.

(4) Measurements of Dealey Plaza

The following measurements are distances in yards from Hoffman's location on the west side of Stemmons Freeway to known landmarks in Dealey Plaza. Two measuring devices were used to calculate these distances. The primary method was with a hand-held laser rangefinder mounted on a tripod. Additional measurements were obtained by utilizing a 300 foot steel measuring tape. Due to the thick growth of trees now currently growing in the area below the railroad embankment, the laser rangefinder was supplemented with the steel tape:

To the railroad bridge	110 yards
To the middle of the triple underpass	180 yards
To the middle switchbox	190 yards
To the man in the business suit	225 yards
To the corner of the picket fence	230 yards
To the railroad switching tower	240 yards

Recall that on the day of the assassination, Stemmons Freeway was only five lanes wide in contrast to seven lanes wide today. Two lanes of highway measure 26 feet (One lane is 13 feet wide). 26 feet (nine yards) was subtracted from each distance to the specific points inside Dealey Plaza, i.e., triple underpass, picket fence, railroad switchbox, and the railroad switching tower.

The authors checked these same distances against the Internet mapping website Google Earth. Comparing the field measurements against the distances provided by Google Earth, a minimum variance of 10 yards and a maximum variance of 18 yards were obtained for each measurement. This variance was likely due to the inability to make exact straight-line measurements in the field due to the existing terrain.

Measurements

In an attempt to estimate the height of the Old Charter billboard and to determine whether or not it interfered with Hoffman's view into the parking lot, measurements were made using photo 60, on page 70. The Secret Service published nine black and white photographs of Dealey Plaza and the surrounding area and used them in their investigation of the assassination. These photographs can be viewed on line at www.historymatters. com.

Using this photo as a base, the height of the billboard was compared photographically to known heights of structures in the immediate area. The photo was taken from a point of less than 150 yards west of the triple underpass.

According to Texas Department of Transportation records (TDOT) the standard height requirement for vehicle clearance under Elm Street was 14 feet. Today, a metal TDOT sign is displayed above Elm Street, showing the height to be 14 feet. Using a cropped version

(Photo 61, on page 71) of the Secret Service photo, a white double arrow has been used to represent that measurement. The solid white line to the right of "ELM" was measured by the authors to be five feet. Adding these two figures gives the total height of the roadway to the top of the railroad embankment, 20 feet. The dotted white line represents the total measurement for this distance.

From the top of the underpass to the top of the concrete railing is nine feet (black double arrow). From the top of the concrete railing to the roadway below is 23 feet (solid white line). The solid horizontal line represents the height of the overpass to the top of the Old Charter billboard. On the day of the assassination, the height of the Old Charter billboard was nearly identical to the triple underpass.

Hoffman has maintained he was able to see several men and one uniformed police officer standing on the triple underpass before, and after the assassination. Since the billboard's height was nearly the same height as the triple underpass, we conclude if Hoffman could see the top of the triple underpass, the Old Charter billboard did not block his view to the east. From Hoffman's position on Stemmons Freeway, the billboard was below his line-of-sight. In addition, the billboard was angled approximately 65 feet from Elm Street, making it even less of a vision obstruction for Hoffman (Photo 64).

In his book, "Case Closed" (1993), Gerald Posner writes,

> "Moreover, in 1963, a large Cutty Sark billboard also filled much of the space between the freeway and the railroad tracks. It is almost impossible for Hoffman to have seen what he described." (P. 258).

In 2007, the authors took measurements of the billboard currently on display on the west side of the triple underpass. At that time, the billboard displayed an advertisement for Shiner Beer (Photos 68 and 71, on pages 74-75). The steel frame of the current billboard is 28 feet north of the Elm Street curb. The sign is anchored in the ground by five steel I-beams and the entire length was measured at 45 feet. Due to the steep grade directly under the sign, the authors could only estimate the distance from the bottom of the sign to level ground at about 15 feet. The current billboard is 14 feet taller than the Old Charter billboard. Sometime between November 22, 1963 and the 1980's, the angle and height of the sign was changed. Additionally, the entire sign was moved closer to the embankment.

The angle of the billboard was set so motorists traveling east on Main and Commerce Streets would have the best view of the advertisement. Motorists traveling west along Main and Elm would see the billboard in their rear-view mirrors.

The white line on Photo 68 (Page 74) shows the angle of the sign in relation to the railroad tracks and Elm Street. Not only was the billboard not parallel to the railroad tracks, it was not parallel to Elm Street.

The authors have concluded the following regarding the billboard and its relevance to the observations made by Ed Hoffman are, (1) the Old Charter billboard was not in Ed Hoffman's line-of-sight; (2) Hoffman's elevated position on Stemmons Freeway was at the same level as the railroad tracks and parking lot on the west side of the book depository; and (3), the angle of the billboard on November 22, 1963 did not block Hoffman's view of the parking lot, the railroad tracks, or the triple underpass.

| H to A-75 |
| H to B-240 |
| H to C-230 |
| H to D-225 |
| H to E-190 |
| H to F-180 |

Photo 86: This aerial view of Dealey Plaza shows the starting point "H" to specific points related to Hoffman's observations of November 22, 1963. All measurements were calculated in yards.

In 1967, FBI agent Udo Specht went with Ed Hoffman to the exact location where he stood during the assassination. Agent Specht writes in his field report:

> The distance from where Mr. Hoffman was viewing the motorcade on Stemmons Freeway to the area behind the wooden fence is estimated at approximately (the number 280 is crossed out and replaced with the numbers 150-200) yards, with the elevation being approximately the same height as the first floor of the Texas School Book Depository.

CONCLUSION

- Ed Hoffman has maintained a freight train moved north across the top of the triple underpass moments after he saw the President's limousine pass his location.

- In his letter to Chief Curry, Officer White stated a train moved north across the tracks at the time of the shooting.

- Officer White told the FBI a train traveled south between his position and Officer Foster's as the motorcade approached the triple underpass.

- During his Warren Commission testimony, White mentioned a passing train but was not asked which direction the train was traveling.

- Officer Foster did not mention a passing train in his December 4th letter to Chief Curry. During his FBI interview, he stated a train moved south across the triple overpass. Foster told author Larry Sneed a train did pass behind him as the limousine approached but did not state which direction this train was moving.

- Officer Brown testified at least one train was moving in the switching yard while he was stationed on the railroad bridge, but was not asked, nor did he volunteer which direction it was moving when he saw it.

- The train seen in Bell's film had to have traveled from south to north when it was recorded on film. Regardless of whether the train was still moving or was stopped when Bell recorded it on film, the fact is in order for this train to be in this position on the railroad bridge, it had to have come from the south.

- The only other explanation for the train to be at this location when it was recorded on Bell's film was the entire length of the train was parked on the tracks between the north end of the triple underpass and the railroad bridge. Once the shooting started, the train started moving north and was crossing over the railroad bridge when Bell filmed it.

- Once the shooting started, the train began moving north across the railroad bridge as Bell filmed it.

- Ed Hoffman's claim of seeing a northbound freight train has been corroborated by the statements of Officer White and the Mark Bell film. The different versions of Officer Foster's observations about a passing train are suspect.

Dazed And Confused

"Agent Griffin no longer has any personal recollection concerning his interview with Mr. Hoffman"

FBI Agent Udo Specht

Ed Hoffman and the FBI

The Warren Commission had completed its work and disbanded by the fall of 1964. Ed Hoffman was never called to provide testimony, and as far as the government was concerned, he did not exist. The images of the gunman at the fence line, and his accomplice, were still fresh in his mind and it haunted him everyday. Ed Hoffman was now more determined to tell the authorities what he had seen.

In the spring of 1967, Ed's supervisor at Texas Instruments, Jim Dowdy, and a coworker, Glenn Bourland, encouraged Ed to contact the FBI. Dowdy called the FBI, and set up the appointment. Ed wondered if the FBI might consider his observations a threat to the official conclusion of a lone gunman in the Book Depository.

On June 26, 1967, Dowdy telephoned the Dallas field office on Ed's behalf. There is no doubt Dowdy told the FBI that the man he was making the appointment for was a deaf mute. The agent to whom Dowdy spoke, Special Agent Will Hayden Griffin, agreed to meet with Ed two days later. According to Griffin's FBI report, Dowdy was instructed to have Ed write his observations on paper and bring it to the interview. There are no handwritten notes from Ed Hoffman in the report filed by Griffin. There are four possible explanations for this; (1) Griffin's request was not communicated to Hoffman by Dowdy; (2) the request was never made by Griffin and his report is incorrect; (3) Ed Hoffman did write his observations on paper and presented them as requested but they were never placed in Ed's official FBI file; or (4) Ed chose not put comply with the agents request.

On June 28, Ed arrived at the Dallas office of the FBI alone. After making contact with the receptionist, he handed her a note, and gestured that he had an appointment. While waiting, he noticed the desk next to the receptionist had a Central Intelligence Agency logo attached to it. Ed knew the CIA was America's top intelligence agency, and gestured to the receptionist his appointment was with the FBI, not the CIA. The receptionist seemed to understand and gestured for Ed to sit down.

FBI Special Agent Will Hayden Griffin ushered Ed into a small room with a table, a couple of chairs, and a large glass mirror along the left wall from where Ed was seated. Agent Griffin had not arranged to have a sign language interpreter present for this interview with Ed Hoffman. Hoffman attempted to tell his story though handwritten notes, crude sketches, and gestures. According to Ed's account, Griffin appeared to listen attentively, and did not ask Ed for clarification on any part of his story. The large mirror on the wall seemed obvious to Ed and he wondered who might be watching from the other side. Griffin sensed Hoffman's discomfort, and gestured assurance that no one was watching.

Without an interpreter present, Griffin may have misunderstood Ed to say he saw two men "running from the rear of the Book Depository." Those who knew Ed's story in 1963, find this statement interesting. On the day of the assassination, Ed became even more concerned when the news reports announced the arrest of Lee Oswald as the man who shot President Kennedy, and how Oswald fired the shots from inside the Texas School Book Depository. Ed knew the Book Depository had nothing to do with what *he* saw.

The official FBI reports of that interview, released under the Freedom of Information Act, are vague and distorted, perhaps because of poor communication or a deliberate attempt to discredit Ed's account. Agent Griffin's report is full of transcription errors, and the only correct information on the report was Hoffman's address, the location where he was standing, his seeing the two men behind the fence, and that he was coming forward with this information against his father's advice.

Griffin's report states, "Hoffman saw two white males clutching something dark to their chests and ran north away from the School Book Depository into the railroad yards." There is no mention in Griffin's report of Ed seeing a weapon, the man who stood by the switchbox, or the puff of smoke. Either Hoffman failed to mention these details during the interview and Griffin misunderstood what Ed was trying to communicate, or, Ed *did* mention these details but Griffin chose not to include it in his report.

It is understandable when someone who is not familiar with sign language attempts to communicate with a deaf person. There is the real possibility of miscommunication and interpretation errors. Agent Griffin knew he was going to interview a deaf person, which is why he supposedly instructed Dowdy to have put his statement on paper.

At the conclusion of the interview, Ed was satisfied he had told Griffin everything he had seen of the man behind the picket fence and of the man at the railroad switch box. Griffin gathered up Ed's notes and sketches, and communicated to Ed using the following gestures,

> A smile while raising an index finger; He points to Ed and brings an index finger up to his lips (as if to say "quiet"); Mimes removing a wallet from his back pocket; mimes giving Ed something small, with one hand; holds up one hand, palm facing Ed, with fingers extended into the number "5"; Griffin closes his hand into a fist, twice (suggesting two zeroes).

According to Hoffman, Griffin did not actually produce any money during the interview, but Ed was shocked by what he understood these gestures to represent. Hoffman gestured he was not interested in money for his testimony, and according to Hoffman, Griffin's demeanor quickly changed into a stern and almost angry expression. Griffin gestured, "You keep quiet about this!" Ed rose to his feet and quickly left the room.

Ed rode the elevator down to the first floor and started to exit the building. While thinking about the sketch he had made for Griffin, he believed he had drawn the fence incorrectly. He turned and went back up to the FBI office and found Agent Griffin. Ed tried to communicate to Griffin the fence had not been drawn to scale and he wanted to correct it. Griffin responded with a "You keep quiet" gesture, and an expression that was angrier than before. Griffin's version of this return visit was,

> Approximately two hours after the above interview with Hoffman, he returned to the Dallas office of the FBI and advised he had just returned from the spot on Stemmons Freeway where he had parked his automobile and had decided he could not have seen the men running because of a fence west of the Texas School Book Depository building. ...He said it was possible that he saw the two men on the fence or something else.

Hoffman has maintained he never made this a statement, and, in fact, was not even aware such a statement had been attributed to him. Without the benefit of an interpreter, this statement may have been the result of misunderstanding between the two men or a deliberate misrepresentation by Griffin.

Ed's gestures were obviously misunderstood again and this is what many of Hoffman's critics cite as proof Hoffman has changed his story. A former intelligence officer suggested to Ed the offer of a bribe may have been an attempt to discredit him. If Hoffman had accepted the money, his motives for offering his statement could have been questioned.

Ten years later, an FBI report on Ed cites Agent Griffin's sudden case of amnesia regarding his interview with Ed,

> SA WILL HAYDEN GRIFFIN, Dallas, Texas interviewed Mr. VIRGIL E. HOFFMAN on 6/28/67, as set forth in Dallas LHM dated 6/28/67. SA GRIFFIN advised SA (Udo Specht's name is blacked out) that he no longer has any personal recollection concerning his interview with Mr. HOFFMAN

Before returning home after the interview with Griffin, Ed stopped at the body shop where Lucien Pierce worked. Hoffman told Pierce about the interview with the FBI and how the agent may have been trying to offer him money. Ed eventually left the body shop and drove to the flower shop.

When Ed entered the floral shop, he saw his father standing at the counter glaring at him. Ed's father asked (in sign language), "Did you go see the FBI?" (Ed had left one of the floral shops business cards in the event Agent Griffin needed to contact him again.) Griffin had called the shop and spoke with Ed's father shortly after Ed left the FBI office. "Yes, I couldn't hold it any longer. Now that I got it out, I feel better." Ed's father told him, "You'll just have to help yourself from now on; I can't do anything about it if they shoot you too!"

Ed had hoped his visit to the FBI would bring him some peace, but it was more trouble than he had expected. Griffin's offer of money, his order telling Ed to keep quiet, and now his father knew he had contacted the FBI. Ed had hoped by contacting the FBI his conscience would be cleared. Instead it brought him more pain and anguish. Having the FBI contact his father upset him horribly.

On July 3, 1967, FBI Director J. Edgar Hoover, sent a message to the Special Agent in Charge of the Dallas field office and ordered the local agents to conduct a follow-up investigation of Ed Hoffman. The memo directed agent to:

> ...fully resolve the matter of Virgil E. Hoffman allegedly seeing two white males running from the rear of the Texas School Book Depository immediately following the assassination of President Kennedy as set out in Dallas LHM 6/28/67.

Hoover also instructed the agents to resolve these four key issues relating to Ed Hoffman and his allegations:

- Whether Ed was interviewed during the initial investigation and if so, did his statement change from the interview of 6/28/67

- Determine if there was a fence located where Ed stated there was in the initial interview.

- Interview Ed's father and determine how much credence should be given to his story.

- Determine if there were other witnesses who saw someone running from the rear of the Book Depository.

It is interesting that FBI agents were directed to interview Ed's father to determine if his son was a credible witness. Was it because he saw a gunman fire from behind the fence and in front of President Kennedy?

It is important for the reader to remember Frederick Hoffman did not want his son talking to the FBI. Ed's father was even reluctant to share his son's story with his brother Robert Hoffman, who was a detective with the Dallas Police Department. Ed's father was deeply concerned about his son's safety so one has to wonder how cooperative he might have been with the FBI. Frederick Hoffman's primary concern was to divert the FBI's attention away from his son to keep him safe.

Ed's younger brother Fred recalls overhearing the interview between his father and FBI Special Agent Udo Specht. Fred Hoffman's version of the interview differs from the information contained in the FBI report. According to Fred, Frederick responded to the agent's questions by saying, "I don't know if Ed saw what he saw." Specht's report states,

> The father of Virgil Hoffman stated that he did not believe that his son had seen anything of value and doubted he had observed any men running from the Texas School Book Depository and for this reason had not mentioned it to the FBI.

Ed's critics often refer to this paragraph of Specht's report as suggesting "his own father thought he was lying." Everyone in the Hoffman family believed the story Ed had told them. It was Frederick's fear for his son's safety which drove his passion to protect Ed.

On July 6, 1967, the FBI interviewed Roy Truly, manager of the Texas School Book Depository, to ascertain whether a fence was located in the area where Ed said he saw the man in the business suit fire a weapon. One has to wonder why the FBI needed to interview Truly when they would have seen the fence had they visited the site. As a result of this interview with Truly, the agents were able to determine the fence did exist. The FBI report states,

> Agents observed a fence approximately 6 feet tall running from the parking lot west of the Texas School Book Depository for about 150 feet to the north of the Texas School Book Depository.

To determine if Hoffman's statement about seeing men running out the back of the Book Depository, FBI agents interviewed three men who had submitted affidavits to the Sheriff's office on the day of the assassination. James Romack, George Rackley and Samuel Pate (it is not known how or why the FBI chose to interview these particular men to corroborate Ed Hoffman's claim). According to the FBI report,

...all three were standing in the rear of the Texas School Book Depository at the time of the assassination. The three people interviewed stated they did not see anyone leave the rear of the Texas School Book Depository immediately after the assassination.

FBI Report 1977

After his father died in 1976, Ed felt compelled to contact the FBI again. Since he had seen nothing come of his first visit, he assumed the agent must have misunderstood what he tried to tell him in 1967. On March 21, 1977, Ed's supervisor at Texas Instruments, Tom Cordner, telephoned the Dallas FBI office and advised that although Ed Hoffman has difficulty in communicating because he is deaf, he (Hoffman) has given indications he knows something about the murder of President Kennedy." An interview was scheduled for April 5, 1977.

This time, Ed enlisted the help of his Texas Instruments supervisor, Richard Freeman, to serve as translator. The two men met with Special Agent Udo H. Specht at the FBI office, located in the Mercantile Continental Building on Commerce Street. Freeman's assistance gave Ed the opportunity to persuade Specht to accompany them to Stemmons freeway where Ed had seen the two men behind the fence. Ed gave Specht his supervisor's business card, and copies of two letters — his own 1975 letter to Senator Ted Kennedy, and the Senator's reply.

Ed recalled later that Agent Specht genuinely seemed to believe what he was telling him regarding the men behind the picket fence. Hoffman was even more encouraged when Specht agreed to go with him to Dealey Plaza. Agent Specht took several pictures from Ed's location on Stemmons freeway. Ed quickly came to the realization the FBI may not believe his story now. As the three men stood on the shoulder of Stemmons Freeway, the view of the backside of the picket fence was partially blocked by trees growing along the railroad embankment. Additionally, the billboard along the embankment had been raised several feet and completely blocked their view into the parking lot on the west side of the Book Depository. Hoffman tried to explain to Agent Specht the trees were taller now and the billboard was not at the same height or location as it was in 1963.

The report filed by Specht states,

> Mr. Hoffman attempted to communicate the same basic information that he previously furnished to the Dallas FBI, as set forth in Dallas FBI memorandum dated June 28, 1967.

> In addition to that information, Hoffman attempted to communicate that he saw two men, one with a rifle and one with a handgun, behind a wooden fence at the moment he saw the presidential motorcade speed north on Stemmons Freeway. Hoffman made hand motions indicating that one of the men disassembled the rifle and placed it in a suitcase or similar container. Hoffman indicated that he saw smoke prior to that. The two men ran north on the railroad tracks and he lost sight of them...

The report continues,

> He tried to get the attention of a Dallas policeman who was standing on the railroad overpass that crosses Stemmons Freeway, but since he could not yell, he could not communicate with the policeman. He drove his car north on Stemmons Freeway after the motorcade passed him in an effort to find the two men, but he lost sight of them.

According to the actual text of the 1977 report, the information contained in it was not taken from Ed at all, but came second-hand, as told by Richard Freeman, in two different phone conversations; one on March 25 and the other three days later.

Even though the FBI recorded both phone conversations of Richard Freeman, there are significant differences between the two reports filed by Agent Specht. The information recorded in the second phone call is more accurate than in the first. In the days between these two phone calls, Freeman went with Ed out to Stemmons Freeway. Freeman was able to see for himself the trees along the railroad embankment now blocked the view into the parking lot on the west side of the Book Depository. The backside of the picket fence and the railroad switch box were totally blocked from view.

Now the FBI had Richard Freeman's version of Ed Hoffman's observations. Information told to one person who then tries to convey the same information to a second person is bound to lose some information. A strong possibility exists some information will be misunderstood or misinterpreted. The report filed by Special Agent Specht contains several relevant errors, some of which were published by assassination researchers as proof Ed Hoffman had changed his story. The 1977 report filed by Agent Specht is Richard Freeman's version of Ed's story and is not accurate.

The FBI report of the March 25 conversation with Freeman states, "Hoffman saw two men, one with a rifle and one with a handgun prior to the arrival of the motorcade." The truth is Ed did not see either of the two men with a gun *prior* to the shooting. To clarify the question of a handgun, Ed saw a handgun in a shoulder holster worn by the man in the business suit at the moment he threw the rifle to the yard man.

The report also provides a clothing description of these two men. Specht writes, "The two men were dressed in some type of white suits and both wore ties." Remember, the agent reporting this information admits in the report he did not get this information directly from Ed Hoffman. This is another example of how Ed's critics suggest he has changed his story.

Another error in this FBI report states that Hoffman saw, "Both men ran north on the railroad tracks." Actually, Ed only saw yardman walk briskly north along the railroad tracks and out of the area. According to Ed, yardman was carrying the dissembled rifle in the tool bag as he left the area. The man in the business suit returned to the fence and mingled with the crowd.

The possibility for significant interpretation errors exist because of the linguistic ambiguity in American Sign Language. Ed Hoffman was not confused about the events he witnessed on November 22nd. The real issue is his unfamiliarity and awkwardness with the English language. This is a skill Ed Hoffman was not taught and has not mastered. His command of the written and spoken word can be compared to a five-year old trying to read, write, and speak a foreign language.

In preparing the 1977 report, FBI Agent Udo Specht went with Ed to Stemmons freeway for the sole purpose of taking pictures. Specht's report states,

> On March 28, 1977, Virgil E. Hoffman accompanied Special Agent [Udo Specht's name is blacked out] to Stemmons Freeway, also known as Interstate Highway 35 North, Dallas, Texas. Special Agent [name blacked out] took color photographs for the area of Stemmons Freeway where Mr. Hoffman was watching the presidential motorcade November 22, 1963. Photographs were also taken of the area north of the grassy knoll where the wooden fence is located, and the area adjacent to it, which is now primarily used as a parking lot...Photographs were taken with a Bessler Topcon camera, using Kodak Vericolor II, Type S film, with a distance setting of infinitive, f Stop 4, and film speed 1/125 a second.

Agent Specht attempts to estimate the distance between Ed's position on the highway to the picket fence on the grassy knoll. He writes,

> The distance from where Mr. Hoffman was viewing the motorcade on Stemmons Freeway to the area behind the wooden fence is estimated at approximately (the number 280 yards is crossed out and replaced with the number (150-200) with the elevation being approximately the same height as the first floor of the Texas School Book Depository building.

It appears the distance between these two points grows and contracts, depending on who does the measuring. Ed's critics often take the farthest measurement to support their view that no one could make out any detail at that distance.

FBI Documentation

The criticism against Ed Hoffman heard most often is he keeps changing his story. These critics allege he told the FBI one version in 1967 and a completely different version in 1977. These are the same critics who insist all of the FBI documents relating to Ed have been released to the public. To this day, none of the handwritten notes or sketches Ed Hoffman made during his 1967 interview with Agent Griffin have been located. Ed claims he drew at least one sketch of the picket fence on a single piece of paper. At the conclusion of the interview, Griffin gathered all of the papers and showed Ed the door. There is no mention of Griffin submitting any notes or sketches with his field report. Normally if an investigator collects this type of evidence from a witness, it is included in the witnesses file for future reference. Specht's report states the Bureau wanted a written statement from Ed Hoffman, but there is nothing in the official record they ever received such a statement. The *only* document of Ed's own composition is a copy of his 1975 letter to Senator Ted Kennedy.

When Ed is told that his critics claim he submitted a "handwritten statement" to the FBI, he explains that his writing skills are such that he is not capable of such a request. He communicates with non-signing people through notes, sketches, and animated gestures. This line from the 1977 FBI report clearly illustrates this point:

On March 21, 1977, Virgil E. Hoffman…voluntarily appeared at the Dallas FBI Office and Special Agent [name of agent blacked out] attempted to communicate with him…Agent [name of agent blacked out] had great deal of difficultly communicating with Mr. Hoffman since he is a deaf mute… and appears to be semi-illiterate in reading and writing of the English language.

Comparing the FBI's assessment of Ed's communication problems from Specht's 1977 report with the very detailed, and very different version in Griffin's 1967 report. There are at least eight different times in the report where it states, "Hoffman said…" In the 1977 report, there is only one, "Hoffman communicated…," which introduces a lengthy narrative of what Ed saw. How did Ed communicate his story to Agent Specht? Two methods are possible: Three days before meeting with Ed, Agent Specht was given an oral translation of his story from Ed's coworker, Richard Freeman or Specht photographed Ed on Stemmons Freeway, at the picket fence and in the parking lot.

The FBI documents on Ed Hoffman that have been declassified and released for public view are as follows:

- Special Agent Will Griffin's 1967 typewritten report of Ed's visit to the Dallas office, and Griffin's interview with Ed's father and brother (that report has been released with no accompanying documentation);

- Special Agent Udo Specht's 1977 typewritten report of Ed's March 25th visit, the March 25th and 28th phone calls from Richard Freeman, and the March 28th Dealey Plaza photo session with Hoffman. This report attaches two documents which Ed submitted to the FBI—the letter he sent to Senator Ted Kennedy in 1975, and the Senator's written response. The report provides no information as to the location of the photos which were taken in preparation of the report;

- Copies of photos, which were released by the federal government in response to a Freedom of Information Act request. The pictures do not include any taken from Stemmons Freeway looking towards the picket fence, nor do they include pictures which Agent Specht took of Ed demonstrating the activity that he saw, which was the basis of the 1977 report.

The FBI's Credibility

The American public has been inclined to give the FBI the benefit of the doubt when trying to assess their reasons for inaccuracies in their field reporting. It is assumed the errors were simply a miscommunication problem between a deaf person and a hearing person. Researchers who have interviewed Ed Hoffman themselves have misinterpreted some details of his story. How much more likely would the FBI reports contain errors, given the fact there were no interpreters present during any of the interviews?

An example of this "wrong reporting" by the FBI occurred in the case of CIA spy Aldrich Ames and his wife in 1994. Immediately after both Ames and his wife were arrested, the FBI released the wife's confession, admitting to all the charges against them. The media published and repeated the confession, but after one week, they discovered the

FBI fabricated the confession. What was the motive in producing a fictitious confession? Was it done to pressure Aldrich Ames into confessing, or was the pressure on the Bureau so great to clear the case they manufactured the "confession?" In either case, we would expect the fraudulent document is still part of the permanent record in their files.

In Ed Hoffman's case, the FBI was still the government's investigative arm in the Kennedy assassination case and had turned in their conclusions years before. What other reason would there be to dismiss Ed's testimony than as the ramblings of a deaf mute? Agent Specht wrote in his 1977 report,

> On pages 71-76 of the Report of the President's Commission on the Assassination of President John F. Kennedy" [sic] the witnesses at the Triple Underpass are discussed, but the Warren Commission's investigation has disclosed no credible evidence that any shots were fired anywhere other than the Texas School Book Depository Building. In the view of the above, the Dallas Office is conducting no additional investigation, UACB.

Even though Agent Specht had perceived Ed's testimony important enough to warrant further personal investigation, Hoover had spoken, and apparently no dissenting view from the rank and file agents was allowed. In other words, no more follow-up.

At this point, several questions must be asked about these reports filed by the Bureau.

- Why is Agent Specht's name blacked out of a field report when Agent Griffin's name is not?

- Why is the Warren Commission Report referred to since Ed Hoffman was never called to testify?

- Why did Specht take pictures of the area if no follow-up investigation was planned?

- What use, if any, was made of those photographs?

- Where are these photos and why were they not included in Specht's field report?

FBI Agent Udo Specht

Author Bill Sloan wrote about Ed Hoffman in more detail in his book, "JFK: Breaking the Silence" (1993). To learn more about Ed's encounter with the FBI, Sloan interviewed FBI Special Agent Udo Specht, who had interviewed Ed in 1977. Referring to the 1977 field report, Sloan asked Specht to explain why the agent's name was blacked out of the 1967 report and why his [Specht's] name was blacked out of his own report.

Specht describes the blacking out of the agents name as one of the bureau's "standard processing procedures." Specht told Sloan, "It is done as a matter of routine to protect the privacy of the agents involved in particular investigations." What is curious is the fact that Agent Griffin's name was on some of the field reports, but missing in other reports.

Specht told Sloan at the time of the assassination, he was not employed with the agency but joined in 1965 and was assigned to Dallas. "I was assigned to be a kind of custodian of the files pertaining to the Kennedy case, he told Sloan." I distinctly remember going out to the site with Mr. Hoffman and I recall I wanted to get a perspective on exactly what could be seen from there."

Because of Ed's agitated mannerisms and excitability, Specht wondered if Hoffman might be suffering from some sort of emotional or psychiatric disorder. Specht told Sloan,

> He [Hoffman] seemed very conscientious and I was convinced he believed what he was saying...but I also know people's minds sometimes register something different from what they've actually seen. Seeds can be planted in a person's mind and may fester over the years into an obsession, and I wondered if there might have been certain factors in his life which could affect his credibility. (P. 43)

In fact, Ed Hoffman has no history of mental or emotional illness. On the contrary, every aspect of his life — his job, his marriage, his finances, his friendships and his personal habits — show nothing but stability.

Specht told Sloan he recalls having considerable difficulty communicating with Hoffman during their interview. Despite these difficulties, Specht said he had doubts about Ed's emotional state but tried to keep an open mind about the allegations. Specht said he even devoted extra effort and time checking into Ed's story. Specht told Sloan he recalls taking photographs from the highway [Stemmons Freeway] and of Ed near the picket fence demonstrating the actions of the man who supposedly fired the weapon at the President. Specht told Sloan after interviewing Hoffman, he "Reported the whole thing to Washington." (Page 43).

Sloan asked Specht how the agents converted their notes to written reports after conducting interviews. According to FBI procedures, once an interview is completed, the notes are turned over to a writer-typist who composes an official memorandum in formal, proper language, with close attention to sentence structure, spelling, grammar and clarity. Then, as a matter of "standard procedure," all of the field notes are destroyed. Outside of the legal community, one would ask why should the original field notes be destroyed? How much space could they take up inside a folder? Regardless, it seems the notes by Ed Hoffman were also destroyed.

The House Select Committee on Assassinations

After Watergate and President Richard Nixon's resignation, Congress commenced an investigation of FBI, CIA, and other intelligence agencies. Along this same time, in 1976, was the first public airing of the color silent movie of the Kennedy assassination taken by witness Abraham Zapruder. Consequently, there were calls for a reinvestigation of political assassinations of the 1960's. In 1976, the House of Representatives created a Select Committee to reopen the investigation of the assassination of President Kennedy and also Martin Luther King, Jr.. For many Americans, especially the 80% who by now believed the assassination of President Kennedy was the result of a conspiracy, the House Select Committee on Assassinations hearings were the opportunity they had waited for. Ed Hoffman shared this hope and assumed he would have his chance to tell his story. He recalled that he thought they would call... "I had everything ready, but I never heard a word from them."

In this new investigation undertaken by the federal government, witnesses were called who presented scientific evidence about the shooting. These scientists examined the echo patterns created by gunfire inside Dealey Plaza. Because of his inability to hear, Ed knew he would not be able to contribute anything to these scientific experiments. However, the scientists were able to confirm at least four shots had been fired at the motorcade, and at least one had come from the direction of the picket fence. This is exactly where Ed had seen the man in the business suit fire a rifle.

Ed believed his testimony would be able to corroborate these scientific findings. Assuming he would be called, he was ready to pack a bag and head to Washington, DC. As the hearings continued into the fall, no request came. He began to suspect that because the FBI publicly disputed the committee's overall conclusions of a shooter at the picket fence, no matter what information he could provide, no one would believe him.

By 1979, the committee issued a preliminary report, concluding the assassination was "probably" the result of a conspiracy. The committee was not able to identify other gunman except Lee Oswald, or the depth of the conspiracy. As the final report went to print, Hoffman sent the committee a certified letter describing what he saw on November 22, 1963, and its importance to the investigation. The committee, whose investigation was opposed by many members of Congress, had exhausted its funding, and was being disbanded when Ed's letter was received.

Several days later, the receipt for his letter arrived, dated January 19, 1979. This was the only response Ed would ever receive.

Ed knew this was his last chance to tell someone who could make a difference. However, many assassination witnesses who had vital information to share with the committee were ignored or overlooked. Many felt the reason was their testimony would have been in direct conflict with the verdict of the Warren Commission.

For the next ten years, Ed Hoffman tried to get someone to listen to his story. While some researchers knew his story through copies of the FBI reports, released through Freedom of Information Act lawsuits, even the more serious assassination researchers had not heard Ed's story in any detail. Only that he was a deaf mute and claimed to have seen suspicious activity behind the picket fence at the time of the shooting.

Sound Bites

"I was standing on the wall as he came by and I kept shooting (filming) and one of the shots hit him in the forehead...it was a horrible thing...he just fell back down into the car."

ABRAHAM ZAPRUDER

JIM MARRS: "CROSSFIRE"

In 1976, Jim Marrs began a teaching a course on the assassination of President John F. Kennedy at the University of Texas at Austin. One of his students told Marrs her deaf parents were friends with Ed and Rosie Hoffman and he should talk to them about the assassination. Jim was the first researcher and author to publish Ed's story and is credited with bringing it to the public in the late 1980's and early 1990's. He reported Ed saw a man dressed in a "dark suit, tie and overcoat," standing behind the fence on the grassy knoll. In his book, "Crossfire: The Plot That Killed Kennedy," (1992) Marrs writes,

> Since Hoffman appears to be the most credible witness and since his story only enforces others who told of gunmen on the grassy knoll, it deserves serious consideration...his story also serves as a vivid commentary on the FBI's failure to follow serious leads and its attempts to intimidate witnesses into silence.

Marrs interviewed Ed Hoffman in 1985, in Dealey Plaza and provided Hoffman a copy of the tape to review. The tape is clear that Marrs was unfamiliar with the process of interviewing a deaf person. Unfortunately, Marrs recruited an uncertified interpreter to translate Ed's account of the events of November 22, 1963. Certified interpreters also make mistakes.

During this interview of Hoffman in Dealey Plaza, a large group of relatives, both hearing, and non-hearing followed Marrs and Hoffman as they wound their way through the Plaza. Many of the bystanders were attempting to explain other details of the story. Under these conditions, it is surprising that Marrs was able to get Ed's personal story.

The following is a small exchange between Ed Hoffman, Jim Marrs and the interpreter,

> **Interpreter:** The other man who fired the gun was in a suit.
> **Marrs:** Did he have an overcoat?
> **Interpreter** (signs): Did he have a coat? (The sign for "coat" also means "jacket")
> **Hoffman:** Yes, a nice coat, (finger spells) the word "suit.
> **Interpreter:** It was a nice overcoat, ah, suit. Nice overcoat.

The issue was Ed *never* mentioned an "overcoat" in this or any other interview, except to deny he saw one whenever he was asked about it. Jim Marrs is an exceptional researcher and has given the American public great insight to the assassination of President Kennedy. His creditability in presenting answers to this crime is remarkable.

NIGEL TURNER: "THE MEN WHO KILLED KENNEDY"

Ten years later, Hoffman was videotaped by Nigel Turner's British production team. Turner produced a five-part series, "The Men Who Killed Kennedy" (1988). Ed's eight-minute sequence can be seen in the section entitled, *The Witnesses*.

Ed was filmed at various locations in and around Dealey Plaza demonstrating the movements of the man in the business suit and yardman from Stemmons Freeway looking back towards the picket fence, at the picket fence, mimicking the movements of the man in the business suit, near the railroad tracks, demonstrating the actions of yardman, and back out on the freeway, looking south towards the railroad bridge that crossed over the top of Stemmons Freeway.

At the conclusion of the filming, Hoffman asked the interpreter if he understood what he was signing? The interpreter had to confess he did not and said he was still learning sign language. Ed asked the young man (using sign language) if he did not understand what he was communicating, what story was he telling Turner?" Embarrassed, the interpreter admitted he had not conveyed all of the details, and embellished other parts of the story on his own. Ed wanted to call Turner's production team and tell them what the interpreter had said, but it was too late; the film was already in postproduction and not available for editing.

The voice track, which was added later to the film, gives the impression that Ed Hoffman speaks in an eloquent, colorful and articulate manner. Unfortunately, the voice-over does not match what Ed was signing for the camera.

The final version of the five-part series was not encoded with closed caption capabilities for the hearing impaired, and no one reviewed the voice track for Ed so he could see the words that were being attributed to him. Had this been done in post-production, Ed would have known his story had been mistranslated again.

Interpretation errors (the voice-over) are found in two different points during Hoffman's sequence. Both errors distort the true facts of Ed's story. At the first error, the voice-over quotes Ed as saying, "the man in the business suit *walked* from the fence to the railroad tracks." Ed has maintained that after firing the rifle, the man in the business suit *ran* along the fence line towards yardman.

The second error in the film's voice-over, quotes Ed as saying "The man who carried the rifle left the area walking slowly down the tracks to the waiting railroad cars." Ed has maintained yardman received the rifle from the man in the business suit, took the rifle apart, placed it into a soft bag, and casually, but quickly, walked north along the railroad tracks and out of his view. What Ed actually signed in those two scenes (describing the man in the business suit, and yardman) was different than what appears on the final version of the video.

The video shot by Marrs in 1985 shows Ed *running* rather than *walking*. Critics point to the difference between the "Turner version" and the "Marrs version" as another change in the story. In reality, Ed saw the business suit man run towards the "yardman" but because of Ed's bad knees, the result of an accident he suffered at his job, and he could not run. When Ed told the story using American Sign Language, he signed the man didn't *walk* but *quickly ran*.

The second major error seen in the Turner video deals with yard man and the rifle. Ed demonstrated how yardman took the rifle apart, how he placed the rifle in the "tool box."

Hoffman finger spells the two words, *T-O-O-L* and *B-O-X*.

He then signed how yardman walked toward the train. Contrary to the voice-over for Ed's mimicking actions of yardman, the video shot by Turner suggests both men ran.

Ed gestured that the man in the business suit tossed the rifle to yardman and *walked casually* back to the fence line and mingled with the crowd. Yard man was last seen walking towards the train in the railroad yard.

Bill Sloan: "Breaking the Silence"

Of all the published accounts of Ed Hoffman's story, the most complete can be found in the book, "JFK: Breaking the Silence," (1993). Sloan spent considerable time with Ed Hoffman, his friends, fellow workers, and family members. Ed had more information than Sloan had time to digest which may account for some gaps in the story. Ed assumes the errors in Sloan's account may be attributed to the interpreter who accompanied Sloan. However, on some details, there are many similarities between Sloan's version and Agent Udo Specht's 1977 field report. On page 17 Sloan quotes Ed,

> I saw the man in the dark suit bend down and pick up something, but I couldn't tell what he was doing. Then the train man came around and squatted down beside the other man for a while. A few seconds later, I saw the businessman raise back up, and I was amazed to see he was holding a gun — a long gun, like a rifle.

Hoffman corrected these statements to say, "The man in the business suit bent down and stood up again almost immediately, appearing to pick something up off the ground." Ed did not know the man was holding a rifle until the shot had been fired and the man turned around and faced Ed's direction. Ed initially assumed the puff of smoke he saw was from the man in the business suits' cigarette.

Sloan includes this sentence, "Then the train man came around and squatted down beside the other man for a while." The timing and action are correct, but the location is not. The "train man" (yardman) squatted for only a few seconds at the switch box. Ed assumes he was getting the bag/case open and ready to receive the rifle from the man in the business suit.

Ed says yardman stayed very close to the switch box until he stepped forward and caught the rifle from the man in the business suit.

Sloan then quotes Ed as saying, "Then I noticed that the train man was armed too. He had a pistol in his hand." Actually, the handgun seen by Ed was in a shoulder holster worn by the man in the business suit. Ed never saw the man in the business suit take this gun out of the holster. Yardman appeared to be unarmed, until he caught the rifle from the man in the business suit.

"Then "suit man" tossed the gun over to the "train man" and started running north into the railroad yards." Actually, the man in the business suit walked casually back east into the parking lot after he tossed the rifle to yardman. After taking the rifle apart, yardman quickly walked north along the railroad tracks and out of Ed's view. The man in the business suit assumed a casual composure and mingled with the crowd that was now in the parking lot.

On page 15, Sloan quotes Ed as saying,

> In the excitement, I didn't think to check my watch...but by the time I got where I wanted to be, I'd say it was probably about ten or fifteen minutes past twelve. I had a great view of the whole west end of downtown, especially Dealey Plaza and the railroad yards adjoining the plaza on the north.

I couldn't hear anything, of course, but I couldn't have had a better view. It was like having a ringside seat, and I was really surprised that there was nobody else there to take advantage of it.

Sloan writes, "People with normal hearing probably would not have found the site nearly so appealing. Most likely, they would have been bothered by the constant roar of traffic on the freeway, and the parade route through Dealey Plaza might have seemed much too far away for comfortable viewing. For Ed, though, it was almost ideal" (p.15).

Sloan then quotes Ed, "I think my vision is much sharper than a hearing person's. Because I concentrate totally on what I'm seeing, and there are no sounds to distract me" (p. 15).

The timing of Ed's visit to his friend's auto body shop is out of sequence as reported by Sloan. It is possible Hoffman told Sloan the story out of sequence, and Sloan may not have been aware of the correct sequence of Ed's story.

Ed has been reluctant to publicly criticize the reports of those who have supported him over the years. Most of the errors can be explained away on inaccurate translations by those individuals unqualified to interpret sign language. Ed does not fault qualified interpreters who make mistakes, but is very concerned when the errors are published without correction. Discrepancies from translation errors damage his credibility for future researchers.

ED'S LETTER TO SENATOR TED KENNEDY

Less than a year after Ed Hoffman's initial interview with FBI Agent Griffin, Senator Robert Kennedy was fatally wounded as he left a rally at the Ambassador Hotel in Los Angeles. By this time, Lyndon Johnson, who succeeded John Kennedy in the White House, had announced he would not run for a second term. Robert Kennedy was virtually assured the Democratic nomination for President.

Like his brother John, Robert was allegedly killed by a lone assassin. For Ed Hoffman, the murder of Senator Kennedy ripped open his emotional wounds. He wondered if this man might be connected to the Dallas tragedy. Ed was upset and emotionally fearful. Talking to his friends at work helped ease some of his pain, but the entire incident drew him into a state of depression which lasted for months.

The United States Congress was in the process of investigating the murder of Senator Robert Kennedy as old allegations lingered for a new investigation into the assassination of President Kennedy. Ed decided to contact the one person who should be the most interested in finding the truth — the surviving Kennedy brother, Senator Ted Kennedy.

Ed knew it was a long shot, but decided to write a letter explaining his account of the President's murder. He hoped Senator Ted Kennedy would be excited to find the truth, and would use his political influence to start a new investigation.

Ed spent several days composing and typing the letter. He revised it several times to ensure his explanation was clear. It was a daunting task for Ed, who writes on a level similar to a grammar school student. (See page 58 for the text of the letter.)

One of Ed's co-workers suggested he contact Dallas District Attorney Henry Wade to help supply Senator Kennedy's address. Ed drove to the court house and was eventually given directions to the District Attorney's office. Ed recalled later, "I got nervous when I saw the big fancy gold letters on the District Attorney's office door and saw him sitting behind a large desk with a cigar in his mouth." Ed's deaf friends told him Henry Wade was a serious and busy man.

Ed entered the District Attorney's office and tried to explain he might be in the wrong place. To his surprise, Henry Wade shook his hand and offered Ed help. Ed requested that the district attorney read his letter. Mr. Wade had one of his secretaries get Senator Kennedy's address, and the letter was mailed that afternoon in Dallas.

Several weeks later — on the twelfth anniversary of President Kennedy's death, Ed received a letter in an official United States Senate envelope.

Ed read the letter, but didn't understand it. He read it again and took it to his father for an explanation. His father explained to him Ted Kennedy had no interest in Ed's account and was satisfied with the Warren Report. Ed's father kept asking him why he was so worried about the assassination. The answer was simple: Ed knew the truth and it was not what was reported in the government's version of the assassination. Regardless of Ted Kennedy's rejection, Ed knew his eyewitness account was the key to unlocking the truth in the murder of President Kennedy.

Seeing Is Believing

"...The Warren Commission's investigation has disclosed no credible evidence that any shots were fired anywhere other than the Texas School Book Depository."

THE WARREN REPORT, PAGE 71

CORROBORATION FOR ED HOFFMAN

Since the assassination, many of the published books on the assassination have estimated the number of witnesses in Dealey Plaza at the time of the shooting. Some researchers report that as few as 100 to as many as 600 were present when the President was murdered. Regardless of the numbers, a significant number of these individuals have been identified from affidavits, actual testimony given before the Warren Commission, or simply from the efforts of dedicated assassination researchers. The following list of witnesses is taken directly from three of the primary sources: affidavits, supplementary reports submitted by law enforcement officers, and Warren Commission testimony.

Almost anyone, including children, can qualify as a witness as long as they can offer useful evidence on the matter at hand. However, the witness must meet the competency test. All evidence including real and documentary forms, must be presented in testimonial form so that the opposite side has the opportunity to cross-examine on that evidence.

The conventional wisdom, particularly among non-lawyers, is that circumstantial evidence is generally less reliable than eyewitness testimony. When lawyers make comments such as "the case is only circumstantial" they may be referring to the fact that the evidence in the case is weak. On the other hand, a strong circumstantial case can be made stronger with the testimony of eyewitnesses can be corroborated by more than one person.

In any criminal investigation, corroboration of information from eyewitnesses is vital. If one witnesses an event or has information that could assist the investigation, that information should be recorded as accurately as possible for use in the overall investigation.

The following listing is of those individuals who were present in Dealey Plaza on November 22, 1963 at the time of the assassination of President Kennedy. Their positions in Dealey Plaza at the time of the shooting are located on the maps at the end of this section and the number preceding the name corresponds to their location on those maps. From their own statements, we can locate their positions in Dealey Plaza at the time of the assassination.

Each of these witnesses listed below provided an affidavit to law enforcement, were interviewed by the FBI, submitted an official report, or gave testimony before the Warren Commission. The source of their information will be noted following their statement.

If the witness provided information to another source, such as a book, the title of the book will be listed. If the witness gave testimony to the Warren Commission, the volume and page number will follow their statement.

Many of the statements provided by the witnesses listed below corroborate the statements and observations made by Ed Hoffman. The observations and actions by these witnesses will be the focus of this chapter. Five specific issues will be examined,

(1) seeing a train,
(2) source of the shots,
(3) activity behind the picket fence before or after the shooting,
(4) smoke on the grassy knoll, and
(5) a rifle inside the Secret Service car.

1. Lee Bowers

Location: In the north tower of the Union Terminal Company, 100 yards north of the picket fence.

Cars driving in the parking lot near the book depository: Between 11:55 and 12:25 pm, Bowers saw three different vehicles enter the parking lot on the west side of the book depository just before the shooting (Affidavit);

Source of the shot/s: "The sounds came either from up against the School Depository Building or near the mouth of the triple overpass but something occurred in this particular spot which was out of the ordinary, which attracted my eye for some reason, which I could not identify." (Warren Commission testimony, Volume 6, p. 286);

Activity behind the picket fence: Towards the mouth of the overpass, there were two men. One man, middle-aged, or slightly older, fairly heavy-set, in a white shirt, fairly dark trousers. Another younger man, about mid-twenties, in either a plaid shirt or plaid coat or jacket. (Volume 6, p. 286);

Train moving in the railroad yard: "Sealed off the area, and I held off the trains until they could be examined, and there was some transients taken on a least one train." (Volume 6, page 287)

2. J. W. Foster-Dallas Police Department

Location: On the triple overpass.

Train moving across overpass: "a freight train had passed headed in a southerly direction and he could not see the west side of the overpass where Patrolman White was stationed" (FBI report)

In his report to Chief Curry, dated December 4, 1963, Foster makes no mention of a passing train before, during or after the shooting. (Commission Exhibit 1358, Volume 22, page 605)

When he testified before the Warren Commission, Officer Foster was not asked about nor volunteered any information about a passing freight train.

In "No More Silence" (1998), Foster told Larry Sneed, "Just prior to the shots, a three-engine locomotive went by, so there wasn't a lot that you could see or hear from up there even though the locomotive had already passed and just the boxcars were going by at the time the motorcade passed through. (p. 212)

3. James C. White, Dallas Police Department

Location: On triple overpass, south and west of Officer Foster's location.

A passing train: "just prior to the arrival of the motorcade and President KENNEDY, a freight train passed moving in a southerly direction and blocked his view of the east side of the overpass." (FBI report)

Train on the triple overpass: In his report to Chief Curry, dated, December 4, 1963, Officer White states, "A Texas and Pacific freight train was traveling North on the railroad tracks between the parade and me. As soon as the train cleared the tracks, to where I could cross to where the search was being made, I went to the location to help block off the building" (Commission Exhibit 1358, Volume 22, page 604)

Train on the triple overpass: "There was a freight train traveling. There was a train passing between the location I was standing and the area from which the procession was traveling, and a big long freight train." Later in his testimony, Officer White stated, "As soon as the train passed I went over on the northwest side of the Depository Building." (Warren Commission testimony, Volume 4, page 254)

4. Sam Holland, Signal Supervisor, Union Terminal Railroad

Location: On the triple overpass.

Smoke on the knoll: "I looked over toward the arcade and trees and saw a puff of smoke come from the trees, the puff of smoke I saw definitely came from behind the arcade through the trees." (Affidavit)

Smoke on the knoll: "...and a puff of smoke came out about 6 or 8 feet above the ground right out from under those trees. And as just about this location from where I was standing you could see that puff of smoke. I have no doubt about seeing that puff of smoke come out from under those trees either. I definitely saw the puff of smoke and heard the report from under those trees." (Warren Commission testimony, Volume 6, page 242)

Source of the shots: "I heard a third report and I counted four shots and about the same time all this was happening, and in this group of trees, like someone had thrown a firecracker, or something out, and that is just about the way it sounded." (Volume 6, page 243)

Weapon in the follow-up car: "After the first shot the secret service man raised up in the seat with a machine gun and then dropped back down in the seat." (Volume 6, page 244)

5. RICHARD DODD, TRACK SUPERVISOR, UNION TERMINAL RAILROAD

Location: On the triple overpass.

Source of the shots: He did not look up and did not know where the shots came from. (FBI report)

Smoke on the knoll: He saw smoke near the bushes and trees at the corner of the wooden fence; "the sound of the shots came from the left and in front of us, toward the wooden fence, and there was a puff of smoke that came underneath the trees on the embankment" "Rush to Judgment" (1966)

6. WALTER WINBORN, SWITCHMAN, UNION TERMINAL RAILROAD

Location: On the triple overpass. Not called to testify.

Source of the shots: Winborn was not able to ascertain exactly where the shots were fired from. (FBI report)

In 1966, Winborn told researcher Stewart Galanor, "Smoke had come out from under the trees on the right-hand side of the motorcade, it looked like haze, like somebody had shot firecrackers, it looked like it was ten feet long and about two or three feet wide."

7. CURTIS BISHOP, UNION TERMINAL RAILROAD

Location: On the triple overpass.

The FBI report makes no reference to the source of the shots.

8. EWELL COWSERT, UNION TERMINAL RAILROAD

Location: On the triple overpass.

The FBI report makes no reference to the source of the shots.

9. ROYCE SKELTON, UNION TERMINAL RAILROAD

Location: On the triple overpass.

The FBI report does not indicate whether Skelton was asked about the origin of the shots.

10. Clemon Johnson, Union Terminal railroad

Location: On the triple overpass

Smoke on the knoll: The FBI report states, "Mr. Johnson stated that white smoke was observed near the pavilion." (FBI report)

11. Austin Miller, Union Terminal railroad

Location: On the triple overpass.

Smoke on the knoll: "I saw something which I thought was smoke or steam coming from a group of trees north of Elm off the Railroad tracks." (Affidavit)

Source of the shots: "About that time I turned and looked toward the... there is a little plaza sitting on the hill. I looked over there to see if anything was there, who threw a firecracker or whatever it was..." (Warren Commission testimony, Volume 6, page 224)

Source of the shots: "Well, the way it sounded like, it came from the, I would say from right there in the car. Would be to my left, the way I was looking at him over toward that incline." (Volume 6, page 225)

12. Frank Reilly, Union Terminal railroad

Location: On the triple overpass.

Source of the shots: "It seemed to me like they come out of the trees on the north side of Elm Street at the corner up there." (Warren Commission testimony, Volume 6, page 226)

13. James Simmons, Union Terminal railroad

Location: On the triple overpass.

Smoke on the knoll: Simmons said he thought he saw exhaust fumes of smoke near the embankment in front of the Texas School Book Depository Building. (FBI report)

14. Nolan Potter, Union Terminal railroad

Location: On the triple overpass.

Smoke on the knoll: "POTTER said he recalls seeing smoke in front of the Texas School Book Depository Building rising above the trees." (FBI report)

15. Thomas Murphy, Union Terminal railroad

Location: On the triple overpass.

Source of the shots: "MURPHY said in his opinion these shots came from a spot just west of the Texas School Book Depository Building." (FBI report)

16. Abraham Zapruder

Source of the shots: "I remember the police were running behind me. Of course, they didn't realize yet, I guess, where the shot came from, that it came from that height, in the line of the shooting. I guess they thought it came from right behind me, I also thought it came from behind me." (Warren Commission testimony, Volume 7, pages 570-571)

17. A.J. Millican

Location: On north side of Elm, between the book depository and the Stemmons Freeway sign.

Source of the shots: "...and then immediately I heard two more shots come from the Arcade between the Book Store and the Underpass, and then three more shots came from the same direction only sounded further back." (Affidavit)

18. William Newman

Location: North sidewalk on Elm.

Newman stated on live television that he saw the President get hit in the side of the head; "Then we fell down on the grass as it seemed that we were in direct path of fire. I thought the shot had come from the garden directly behind me, that was on an elevation from where I was as I was right at the curb." (WFAA-TV)

The FBI report states, "He [Newman] suddenly realized they (the President and Governor Connally) had been shot and that he was perhaps in the line of fire because officers started running toward the arcade directly back of him and his wife." (FBI report)

19. Ochus Campbell

Location: Standing in front of the book depository.

Source of the shots: "I heard shots fired from a point which I thought was near the railroad tracks located over the viaduct on Elm Street." (FBI report)

20. Emmett Hudson

Location: On the steps between Elm Street and the picket fence.

Source of the shots: "The shots that I heard definitely came from behind and above me." (Affidavit)

Source of the shots: "...you could tell the shot was coming from above and kind of behind...well, it sounded like it was high, you know, from above and kind of behind like in other words, to the left." (Warren Commission testimony, Volume 7, page 563)

21. Dolores Koumae

Location: Southwest corner of Elm and Houston.

Source of the shots: "She stated there were three of these noises which she now knows were shots equally spaced by a few seconds and that it sounded as though these shots were coming from the Triple Underpass; she did not look up at the Texas School Book Depository Building." (FBI report)

22. Julia Ann Mercer

Location: Between triple overpass and Stemmons freeway ramp.

Suspicious activity prior to shooting: "States she observed a white male carry a gun case and walk up the hill towards the overpass. This individual was between 20 and 30 years of age wearing a gray jacket, brown pants and a plaid shirt." (Affidavit)

23. Jean Newman

Location: On the north side of Elm on the north side of the Stemmons freeway sign.

Source of the shots: "The first impression I had was that the shots came from my right." (Affidavit)

Source of the shots: "NEWMAN stated that when she realized the reports were shots she immediately turned and looked up the hill to the north toward the parking lot." (FBI report)

24. Malcolm Summers

Location: South side of Elm, across from the Newman family.

Source of the shots: "Everyone was running towards the railroad tracks." (Affidavit)

25. Jack Franzen

Location: On south side of Elm, 20 feet west of Malcolm Summers.

Source of the shots: "Because of the activity, FRANZEN presumed the shots which were fired came from the shrubbery or bushes toward which officers appeared to be running." (FBI report)

26. J.C. Price

Location: On top of the Terminal Annex Building (Commerce & Houston)

Activity behind the picket fence: "I saw one man run towards the passenger cars on the railroad siding after the volley of shots. This man had a white dress shirt, no tie and khaki (sic) colored trousers. His hair appeared to be long and dark and his agility running could be about 25 years of age. He had something in his hand. I couldn't be sure but it may have been a head piece." (Affidavit)

27. W.W. Mabra, Dallas County Deputy Sheriff

Location: In front of the Criminal Courts building.

Source of the shots: "I went to the rail yards and parking area west of the book store." (Supplementary report submitted to Sheriff Decker)

28. Harold Elkins, Dallas County Deputy Sheriff

Location: In front of the sheriff's office.

Source of the shots: "I immediately ran to the area from which it sounded like the shots had been fired. This is an area between the rail yards and the Texas

School Book Depository which is east of the railroad." (Supplementary report submitted to Sheriff Decker)

29. J. L. Oxford, Dallas County Deputy Sheriff

Location: In front of the sheriff's office.

Source of the shots: "We ran across Houston Street and across Elm and down to the underpass. We jumped the picket fence which runs along Elm Street and on over into the railroad yards. When we got over there, there was a man who told us that he had seen smoke up in the corner of the fence." (Supplementary report submitted to Sheriff Decker)

30. Luke Mooney, Dallas County Deputy Sheriff

Location: In front of the sheriff's office.

Source of the shots: "I started running across Houston Street and down across the lawn to the triple overpass and up the terrace to the railroad yards.". Mooney testified before the Warren Commission that he believed the shots were coming from the area of the railroad yards at the street level." (Warren Commission testimony, Volume 3, page 282)

31. Roger Craig, Dallas County Deputy Sheriff

Location: In front of the sheriff's office.

Source of the shots: "At the report of the first shot, I started running around the corner of Houston and ran up the terrace on Elm Street and into the railroad yards." (Supplementary report submitted to Sheriff Decker)

Source of the shots: "I continued running across Houston Street, across the parkway, across Elm Street and, by this time, the motorcade had went on down Elm Street and I ran up to the railroad yard and started to look around when the people began to all travel over that way. As I reached the railroad yard, I talked to a girl getting her car that thought they came from the park area on the north side of Elm Street." (Warren Commission testimony, Volume 6, pages 260-270)

32. Buddy Walthers, Dallas County Deputy Sheriff

Location: In front of sheriff's office.

Source of the shots: "I immediately started running across Houston Street and ran across Elm Street and up into the railroad yards." (Supplementary report submitted to Sheriff Decker)

Source of the shots: "...a lot of people was [sic] sitting there, but it must have been behind that fence; there's a fence right along here." (Warren Commission testimony, Volume 7, page 105)

33. Seymour Weitzman, Dallas County Deputy Sheriff

Location: In front of the sheriff's office.

Source of the shots: When asked for a location of the shots, he stated, "It would be between the railroad overpass and I can't remember the name of that little street that runs off Elm, its cater-corner the section there between the monument section."

Deputy Weitzman was asked if he spoke to any railroad employees during his search of the railroad yards. He was asked, "Did the yardman tell you where he thought the noise came from?" Weitzman replied, "Yes, sir; he pointed out the wall section where there was a bunch of shrubbery and I believe that's to the right where I went over the wall where the steampipe was." (Warren Commission testimony, Volume 7, page 107)

Activity behind the picket fence: Weitzman told the Warren Commission that he observed a man carrying Secret Service identification while searching the parking lot.

34. Eugene Boone, Dallas County Deputy Sheriff

Location: In front of the sheriff's office.

Source of the shots: "I ran across Elm Street and up the embankment (sic) over the retaining wall and into the freight yard." (Supplementary report submitted to Sheriff Decker)

35. L. C. Smith, Dallas County Deputy Sheriff

Location: In front of the sheriff's office.
Source of the shots: "I ran as fast as I could to Elm Street, just west of Houston, and the shots came from the fence on the North side of Elm. I went at once behind the fence and searched the parking lot." (Supplementary report submitted to Sheriff Decker)

36. Charles Player, Dallas County Deputy Sheriff

Location: In front of the sheriff's office.

Source of the shots: "I drove my car on to the railroad tracks." (Supplementary report submitted to Sheriff Decker)

37. Harry Weatherford, Dallas County Deputy Sheriff

Location: In front of the sheriff's office.

Source of the shots: "I heard a loud report, which I thought was a railroad torpedo, as it sounded as if it came from the railroad yards. By this time I was running towards the railroad yards where the sound seemed to come from." (Supplementary report submitted to Sheriff Decker)

38. L. C. Todd, Dallas County Deputy Sheriff

Location: Standing on Houston Street, near Main.

Source of the shots: "I immediately recognized them (rifle shots) as being gun fire. I ran across the street and went behind the railroad tracks." (Supplementary report submitted to Sheriff Decker)

39. A. D. McCurley, Dallas County Deputy Sheriff

Location: In front of the sheriff's office.

Source of the shots: "I rushed towards the park and saw people running towards the railroad yards beyond Elm Street and I ran over and jumped a fence." (Supplementary report submitted to Sheriff Decker)

40. Jack Faulkner, Dallas County Deputy Sheriff

Location: In front of the sheriff's office.

Source of the shots: "I asked a woman where the shots came from, and she pointed toward the concrete arcade on the east side of Elm St." (Supplementary report submitted to Sheriff Decker)

41. Senator Ralph Yarborough

Location: Two cars behind President Kennedy's limousine on Elm.

Weapon in the Secret Service car: "After the shooting, one of the secret service men sitting down in the car in front of us pulled up an automatic rifle or weapon and looked backward, until the automatic weapon was uncovered, I had been lulled into a sense of hope." (Warren Commission testimony, Volume 7, page 439)

Smoke on the knoll: When interviewed for the Dallas Times Herald, Yarborough stated, "We smelled gunpowder as we traveled through the plaza."

42. James Tague

Location: At the east end of the underpass between Main and Elm.

Source of the shots: "I thought they were coming from my left; my first impression was that up by the, whatever you call the monument, or whatever it was." (Warren Commission testimony, Volume 7, page 556)

43. D. V. Harkness, Sergeant, Dallas Police department

Location: Corner of Elm and Houston.

Source of the shots: "I went west on Main to observe the area between the railroad tracks and Industrial." (Warren Commission testimony, Volume 6, page 308)

44. Arnold Rowland

Location: On west side of Houston, between Elm and Main.

Source of the shots: When asked if he ever looked back at the book depository, he stated, "No, I did not. In fact, I went over toward the scene of the railroad yards myself." (Warren Commission testimony, Volume 7, page 180)

45. Joe Molina, Texas Book Depository employee

Location: On steps of TSBD.

Source of the shots: "Sort of like it reverberated, sort of kind of came from the west side, that was the first impression I got." (Warren Commission testimony, Volume 6, page 369)

46. ROY KELLERMAN, UNITED STATES SECRET SERVICE

Location: Front passenger seat, Presidential limousine.

Weapon in the follow-up car: "Yes, sir, in this follow-up car we have what is now known as an AR-15." (Warren Commission testimony, Volume 5, page 68)

47. CLINT HILL, UNITED STATES SECRET SERVICE

Location: Driver's side running board of the follow-up car.

Weapon in follow-up car: When asked if there was any other weapons in the car, Hill stated, "Yes. There is an AR-15, which is an automatic rifle, and a shotgun." (Warren Commission testimony, Volume 2, page 134)

48. VICTORIA ADAMS

Location: 4th floor of the book depository.

Source of the shots: "It seemed as if it came from right below rather than from the left above." (Warren Commission testimony, Volume 6, page 387)

49. BILLY LOVELADY, TEXAS SCHOOL BOOK DEPOSITORY EMPLOYEE

Location: Front steps of TSBD.

Source of the shots: "Right there around that concrete little deal on that knoll, between the underpass and the building right on that knoll." (Warren Commission testimony, Volume 6, page 337)

50. MARRION BAKER, DALLAS POLICE DEPARTMENT

Location: On Houston approaching Elm.

Source of the shots: "I think everyone at that time thought these shots came from the railroad track." (Warren Commission testimony, Volume 3, page 259)

51. Edgar L. Smith, Dallas Police Department

Location: Houston and Elm.

Source of the shots: "I ran over there (indicating the railroad yards) and checked back of it." He was then asked, "Toward the railroad tracks there?" Smith responded, "That's true." (Warren Commission testimony, Volume 7, page 567)

52. Clyde Haygood, Dallas Police Department

Location: Motorcycle officer riding several cars behind the Presidential limousine.

Source of shots: "Some of them (eyewitnesses on north side of Elm) were pointing back up to the railroad yard, and a couple of people were headed back up that way. I left my motor on the street and ran to the railroad yard." (Warren Commission testimony, Volume 6, page 297)

53. Earle Brown, Dallas Police Department

Location: Assigned to the railroad bridge over Stemmons Freeway.

Officer Brown told the Warren Commission that "...right after the shots were fired, I smelled gunpowder." (Warren Commission testimony, Volume 6, page 233)

*It is difficult to understand how Officer Brown could have smelled gunpowder if he was stationed on the railroad bridge over Stemmons Freeway some 100 yards north and west of the parking lot. The authors believe Officer Brown was actually closer to the triple overpass rather than at his assigned post on the railroad bridge when the assassination took place. This would explain why Ed Hoffman only saw one uniformed officer on the railroad bridge after the President's vehicle passed his location on Stemmons Freeway.

Trains moving in the rail yard: When Brown was asked if he observed anyone in the railroad yards, he stated, "Not that I recall; now they were moving trains in and out." Later he was asked if his view of the railroad yard was blocked, Warren Commission Counsel Joseph Ball asked, "Was that because of the moving trains?" Brown replied, "Yes." (Warren Commission testimony, Volume 6, page 233)

Weapon in Secret Service car: "...he had this gun and he was swinging it around, looked like a machine gun." (Warren Commission testimony, Volume 6, page 233)

54. Joe Marshall Smith, Dallas Police department

Location: Elm and Houston.

Source of the shots: "...and this woman came up to me and she was just in hysterics. She told me, 'They are shooting the President from the bushes,' so I immediately proceeded up there." Later Officer Smith states, "I checked all the cars." (in the parking lot in the railroad yard) Later Smith stated, "...it sounded to me like they may have come from this vicinity here." (Warren Commission testimony, Volume 6, page 534)

Activity behind the picket fence: "I believe one Secret Service man when I got there...I pulled my pistol from my holster, and I thought, 'this is silly, I don't know who I am looking for,' and I put it back. Just as I did, he showed me that he was a Secret Service agent...he saw me coming with my pistol and right away he showed me who he was." (Warren Commission testimony, Volume 6, page 535)

55. Ronald Fischer

Location: Elm and Houston.

Source of the shots: "They appeared to be coming from just west of the School Book Depository Building. There were some railroad tracks and there were some railroad cars back there." (Warren Commission testimony, Volume 6, page 195)

56. Bobby Hargis, Dallas Police department

Location: Riding in motorcade along left rear of Presidential limousine.

Source of the shots: "...at the time there was something in my head that said that they probably could have been coming from the railroad overpass." I ran across the street looking over towards the railroad overpass." (Warren Commission testimony, Volume 6, pages 293-294)

57. Jean Hill

Location: South side of Elm.

Source of the shots: "I frankly thought they were coming from the knoll. This is a hill and it was like they were coming from right there. I had always thought that they came from the knoll. I thought it was just people shooting from the knoll. I did think there was more than one person shooting, as I said, I thought they were coming from the general direction of that knoll." (Warren Commission testimony, Volume 6, pages 211-212)

(To fully appreciate Ms. Hill's statement, her testimony should be read in its entirety.)

58. Roy Truly, Texas School Book Depository superintendent

Location: Curb in front of the book depository.

Source of the shots: "The sounds came from the direction of the concrete monument next to the wooden fence." (Warren Commission testimony, Volume 3, page 215)

59. Robert West, Dallas County Surveyor

Location: Near the intersection of Main and Houston.

Source of the shots: West told JFK researcher Jim Marrs that the shots sounded as if they were coming from "northwest quadrant of Dealey Plaza." ("Crossfire," page 20)

60. Otis Williams, TSBD credit manager

Location: Front steps of the book depository.

Source of the shots: "The shots were coming from the direction of the overpass." (Affidavit)

61. Phil Willis

Location: Just west of Houston on south side of Elm.

Source of the shots: Texas School Book Depository (Volume VII, pae 496; Right side of Elm Street. (Clay Shaw Trial, 1969); When interviewed by Nigel Turner, Willis stated, "No one will ever convince me that that last shot did not come from the right front, from the knoll area." He stated on camera that the Commission only wanted to hear that shots came from the depository. (Video "The Men Who Killed Kennedy," 1992)

62. STEVEN WILSON, TEXAS SCHOOL BOOK DEPOSITORY EMPLOYEE

Location: 3rd floor of TSBD, 2nd window from the east corner.

Source of the shots: "The shots came from the west end of the building or from the colonnade below me on Elm, across from the west end of our building. The shots did not sound like they came from above me." (FBI report)

63. MARY WOODWARD, "DALLAS MORNING NEWS" REPORTER

Location: Standing on north curb of Elm, just west of the Stemmons Freeway sign.

Source of the shots: Woodward wrote a story for the next day's paper and it that article she wrote, "Suddenly there was a horrible, ear shattering noise from behind us and a little to the right." However, Woodward's editor refused to publish her story.

64. MAGGIE BROWN, DALLAS MORNING NEWS REPORTER

Location: Standing next to Mary Woodward.

Source of the shots: Told JFK researcher Jim Marrs the shots came from behind her and to the right.

65. ELSIE DORMAN, TEXAS SCHOOL BOOK DEPOSITORY EMPLOYEE

Location: 4th floor of book depository.

Source of the shots: "I thought at the time that the shots or reports came from a point to the west of the building." (FBI report)

66. WAYNE AND EDNA HARTMAN

Location: On Main just east of Houston.

Source of the shots: "Shots sounded like they were coming from the bushes near the railroad on the north side." (Affidavit)

67. Roy Lewis, Texas School Book Depository employee

Location: Front steps of book depository.

Source of the shots: "Everyone starting running toward the knoll, but no way did I suspect anything coming from the TSBD." (FBI report)

68. Cheryl McKinnon

Location: On north side of Elm, between curb and pergola.

Source of the shots: "After the shots were fired, I turned towards the knoll, puffs of smoke were still hanging in the air in small patches, but no one was visible." (WFAA-TV appearance, November 22, 1963)

69. Sam Paternostro, Dallas County Assistant District Attorney

Location: 2nd floor, Criminal Courts building.

Source of the shots: "...a shot come (sic) from the depository or the criminal courts building or the triple overpass." (FBI report)

70. William Shelly, book depository manager

Location: Front steps of book depository.

Source of the shots: "...came from west of the depository." (FBI report)

71. Gordon Arnold

Location: North side of Elm, between curb and picket fence.

Source of the shots: Arnold told Nigel Turner that the first shot whistled by his left ear and he immediately threw himself on the ground (Video "The Men Who Killed Kennedy," 1992)

Arnold told JFK researcher Henry Hurt that he felt as if he were standing there under the muzzle. ("Reasonable Doubt," 1985)
Arnold told Earl Gotz in 1978, "The shot came from behind me only inches over my left shoulder, it was being fired right over my head."

72. JOE MURPHY, DALLAS POLICE DEPARTMENT

Location: On Stemmons Freeway over the Elm Street entrance ramp.

Source of the shots: "I was looking in an easterly direction." (Warren Commission testimony, Volume 6, pages 256-260)

73. JAMES LOMAX, DALLAS POLICE DEPARTMENT

Location: Officially stationed on the railroad bridge over Stemmons Freeway.

Officer Lomax did not submit any written report on his activities relating to the assassination.

74. ED HOFFMAN

Location: On Stemmons Freeway.

75. VIRGIE RACKLEY, BOOKKEEPER, TEXAS SCHOOL BOOK DEPOSITORY

Location: Standing on south side of Elm across from the book depository.

Source of the shots: "It sounded as though these sounds were coming from the direction of the Triple Underpass." (FBI Report)

76. MRS. JAMES REESE, OFFICER MANAGER AND ADMINISTRATIVE SECRETARY, TEXAS SCHOOL BOOK DEPOSITORY

Location: Standing on the steps of the book depository.

Source of the shots: "She thought the shots came from the alcove near the benches and then saw people looking up near the building and had presumed the shots had come from the building." (FBI report)

77. BEVERLY OLIVER

Location: South side of Elm, behind Jean Hill & Mary Moorman.

Source of the shots: "The whole back of his head went flying out of the car. Someone was shooting from across Elm by that fence." (Personal interview, 1992)

78. Hollis B. McLain, Dallas Police Department

Location: In motorcade, on Houston approaching Elm Street.

Source of the shots: Officer McLain told the authors that he believed the shots were coming from the area of the triple underpass.

The reader may be familiar with the government's claim that Officer McLain's radio microphone was stuck open when the shots were fired at the President which was recorded on the police audio tapes.

In November 2007, the authors interviewed Officer McLain at the JFK Lancer "November in Dallas Conference." Officer McLain denied that his microphone was stuck open. "I heard the Chief (Jesse Curry) say over the radio to get us to the hospital. If my mike was stuck open, I wouldn't have heard that. They were looking for a scapegoat on that one, my mike wasn't stuck open."

When asked where he was located in the motorcade when the shots were fired, he said, "I was on Houston about halfway between Main and Elm. I was moving straight towards the book depository when I heard the shots." Officer McLain stated that his initial impression was that the shots were coming from the area of the triple overpass, not from the building. "They (the shots) sounded closer to street level than anywhere else."

Officer McLain said that when he heard Curry's directive to proceed to the hospital, he accelerated and tried to catch up to the front of the motorcade. He didn't see the Presidential limousine until it pulled into the emergency entrance to Parkland hospital. As he walked up to the limousine, Mrs. Kennedy was still holding onto the President and was refusing to let the agents remove him from the car. McLain said he reached over the car and grabbed Mrs. Kennedy by the shoulders and picked her up so the President could be removed.

McLain told the authors that sometime in January the next year, he was summoned to police headquarters to talk to FBI agents. When he arrived at the station, all of the motorcycle officers who rode in the motorcade were assembling in a conference room. Two FBI agents entered the room and told the officers that their investigation had determined that all the shots were fired from the Texas School Book Depository and no other place.

McLain said the statement was not open for debate and the agents said that if any of officers believed anything to the contrary, they were simply mistaken. McLain said, "We sure as hell weren't going to sit there and listen to these federal boys tell us what happened during that shooting, so we all got up and walked out on them."

The Truth About Lies

"The truth of Kennedy's death should have been public domain from 12:30 pm, November 22, 1963. That truth, however shocking it might have been then, would have been far less painful than more than four decades of uncertainty and governmental interference."

WALT BROWN, PH.D.

Gerald Posner's "Case Closed"

One of the more vocal of Ed's critics has been Gerald Posner. In 1993, Posner, a former Wall Street lawyer turned assassination researcher, produced a "lone assassin, no conspiracy" rehash of the Warren Commission Report, entitled, "Case Closed." Reviewer David Wise had this to say about Posner's book,

> At last the voice of sanity…a long-awaited, much needed antidote to the conspiracy theorists. "Case Closed" is brilliantly researched, utterly convincing, and compelling. If you read only one book on the assassination, let it be this.

Reading the entire inside cover text gives one the impression this book is as important as the King James Bible.

> After thirty years, "Case Closed" finally succeeds where hundreds of other books and investigations have failed — it resolves the greatest murder mystery of our time.

> "Case Closed" cuts through three decades of misinformation and distortions by examining all the evidence to make sense of what really happened.…and in the process answers the riddle of how and why Lee Harvey Oswald killed JFK.

Fredric Dannen wrote this about Posner's work,

> This book really does close the case. There can now be no doubt that Lee Harvey Oswald alone killed President Kennedy. His reporting meets the highest standards…a great achievement in contemporary journalism.

In his book, Posner wrote, "As in every famous case, people have come out of the woodwork for their fifteen minutes of fame." An examination of several chapters in "Case Closed," should give the reader an opportunity to determine if Posner, himself, is one of those people coming out of the woodwork for his fifteen minutes of fame.

Since Posner was new to the Kennedy investigation, he used other "lone assassin, no conspiracy" supporters for assistance on some of the more complex areas of the case. In fact, in the 506 pages of his work, he cites 1,452 footnotes, and credits 60 different authors for supporting information. Posner's work will be examined in detail to determine if he deserves the praises given for his work.

In "Case Closed," Gerald Posner devotes only *two* paragraphs to Ed Hoffman's story. On page 257, Posner writes, "Hoffman said he was on the Stemmons Freeway, some 250-300 yards west of the picket fence." Posner's source for this sentence was an "interview with Jim Moore," writer of "Conspiracy of One" (1992), another "lone assassin, no conspiracy" author. However, Ed Hoffman's location on the west side of Stemmons Freeway to the east boundary of the picket fence is 230 yards. Why did Posner add an extra 70 yards to the total distance? For an author claiming to clear up false assumptions, it would seem he would want to have the exact measurements before dismissing this witness.

In the next sentence on page 257, Posner writes,

"Unaware that shots had been fired, he claimed to see a man in a suit and tie in the railyard behind the grassy knoll. He was running with a rifle. That gunman then tossed the rifle to a man disguised as a railyard worker and the second man disassembled the rifle, put it into a sack, and walked away."

Close, but again, not accurate. Hoffman stated he saw the railyard worker put the rifle into a toolbox or tool bag, not a sack. Posner cites Jim Marrs' book "Crossfire" as his source for this information. A source that should have been quoted precisely.

Posner then inserts a footnote to this statement,

"Even those who support Hoffman's story find it difficult to explain how anyone was able to disassemble the rifle in the railyard when more than a dozen people ran into that *exact location* (emphasis added) less than a minute after the last shot."

Is Posner referring to the "location" near the middle switchbox where yardman caught the rifle? Ed Hoffman's account states the man with the rifle ran along the fence line and tossed the rifle to yardman. The distance between the man in the business suit and yard man is approximately 35 yards. Running this distance would have taken approximately five to six seconds; add another three to four seconds to break the rifle down and quickly leave the area.

The presidential limo was probably still in Dealey Plaza, and may have been slowing down, or completely stopped, as many witnesses have claimed. The men standing on the triple underpass have not moved from this location.

Witnesses in Dealey Plaza began running into the railroad yard after the last shot and the presidential limousine passed under the triple overpass. The man in the business suit had just been confronted by the uniformed police officer and was mingling with those who rushed into the parking lot. Yardman was walking north out of the area by this time. The primary focus was the picket fence, not the railroad yard.

Posner's next paragraph on page 258 states,

"Hoffman said that when he saw the wounded President speed past in the motorcade, he ran down the grassy incline from the freeway and tried to communicate to a policeman, who did not understand him."

Posner's source for this information is also taken from page 83 of "Crossfire," where Jim Marrs writes,

"Upset over what he had seen, Hoffman looked around for help. He saw a Dallas policeman standing on the railroad bridge crossing Stemmons and he walked toward him waving his arms in an attempt to communicate what he had seen. However, the policeman, unable to understand, simply waved him off."

The translation problems between Ed Hoffman and Jim Marrs have been addressed previously. Misinterpretation of Hoffman's story was relayed through Marrs by a interpreter at the scene. This miscommunication resulted in some spotty, incorrect information as Marrs was explaining what the interpreter thought Hoffman was describing.

When the limousine carrying President Kennedy passed below *this* elevated position, Hoffman saw the damage to the back of the President's head. As Hoffman began running towards the railroad bridge, he was startled by a Secret Service agent in the follow-up car who was pointing a rifle directly at him.

Ed's attempt at "communication with a policeman" consisted of waving his arms and running toward the railroad bridge. The truth is Hoffman never spoke to any law enforcement official, local or federal, on November 22, 1963.

Posner's next paragraph is from information contained in Agent Will Griffin's 1967 FBI report. Posner writes,

> He (Hoffman) said he saw two men running from the rear of the Texas School Book Depository, but the FBI concluded he could not have seen them from where he was because a fence west of the Depository blocked his view. He then changed his story to say he saw the men on top of the fence.

The last sentence of this paragraph is another example of Posner's use of incorrect and misleading information. Posner's source for this sentence is the Warren Commission testimony from Dallas police officer Earle Brown. He writes,

> "Dallas policeman Earle Brown, who was stationed as security on top of *Stemmons Freeway* (author's emphasis) said there was no civilian there." (Volume 6, page 236)

When Officer Brown was questioned by Warren Commission counsel Joseph Ball, Brown attempted to clarify where he was that day,

> **Mr. Brown:** There's one there, too, but that overpass is actually a road. Where I was was the railroad overpass.
> **Mr. Ball:** The railroad overpass itself?
> **Mr. Brown:** Yes, sir.
> **Mr. Ball:** How far were you from the place where the continuation of Elm goes under the overpass?
> **Mr. Brown:** Oh, approximately 100 yards.
> **Mr. Ball:** Now, this is the place where the railroad yards run over the highway?
> **Mr. Brown:** Yes.

Posner misrepresented Officer Brown's testimony to support his contention of another person on Stemmons Freeway who did not see Hoffman. Nowhere in Officer Brown's testimony does he say he was "on top of Stemmons Freeway." *Ed Hoffman* was on Stemmons Freeway. Officer Brown was stationed on the Texas and Pacific railroad bridge, over Stemmons Freeway.

Posner completely misrepresented what the witness testified to under oath. Posner's version of Brown's own testimony suggests to the reader the officer was actually standing *on* Stemmons Freeway, which was not true. According to the Dallas police duty assignment report, two uniformed officers were assigned to the railroad bridge over Stemmons Freeway; Officers Earle Brown and James Lomax.

Anyone who is familiar with the physical layout of Dealey Plaza and the surrounding area should be able to locate Officer Brown's position from his testimony. Officer Brown knew better than anyone that he wasn't *on* Stemmons Freeway. Being "on top of Stemmons Freeway" is completely different than "Where I was was on the railroad overpass." How could Posner have made such a mistake?

Posner continues,

> "Three other policemen on three-wheeled traffic cycles were near where Hoffman claimed to be. They did not see him."

His source for this statement is the Warren Commission testimony of Dallas police Officer Joe Murphy, Volume 6, pages 256-58.

> **Mr. Ball:** Were there any other officers on that overpass?
> **Mr. Murphy:** Yes; there were two more about — oh, a 100 feet south of to slow traffic or to stop traffic whenever the motorcade entered the Stemmons Freeway north entrance.
> **Mr. Ball:** Now where were they located — and, did they as the motorcade came down Elm Street, did they go into the highway and stop traffic?
> **Mr. Murphy:** Yes, they did.
> **Mr. Ball:** Will you put their positions on the Stemmons Freeway overpass at the time the motorcade came west on Elm, and mark it (2) and (3)?
> **Mr. Ball:** Do you know the names of those officers that were (2) and (3.)
> **Mr. Murphy:** I can't recall. I know them but I can't recall who they were.
> **Mr. Ball:** Were they three-wheeler officers too, do they drive three-wheelers?
> **Mr. Murphy:** I believe both of them three-wheelers.
> **Mr. Ball:** And as the motorcade came west on Elm, did they stop traffic on Stemmons freeway?
> **Mr. Murphy:** Yes, their main job was to slow it and let the officers farther down the freeway — they would stop it, but traffic approaches pretty fast and they were to slow traffic and let the officers then stop it. They did — they — they stepped into and were slowing the traffic as the motorcade came under that railroad overpass.
> **Mr. Ball:** Did they ever stop traffic completely?
> **Mr. Murphy:** Well, it stopped — it stopped itself back down when all the excitement — someone down there — they blocked the whole street and then it backed up, is what it did — backed up to our position.
> **Mr. Ball:** On Stemmons Freeway?
> **Mr. Murphy:** Yes.

Photo 87 is a sketch drawn by Officer Joe Murphy during his appearance before the Warren Commission The sketch was marked as Murphy Exhibit A and appears in Volume 20 on page 638. Officer Murphy located his position with an "X" and the letters "Pos. 1" (arrow).

During his testimony, he was asked to locate where the other two officers were located on Stemmons Freeway. Murphy marked their positions with "X's" and the letters "Pos. 2" and "Pos. 3." (dashed line circle).

The "three other policemen on three-wheeled traffic cycles" Murphy mentions during his testimony that were further south on Stemmons Freeway, are not listed in the police duty assignments prepared by Captain Lawrence (Lawrence Exhibit 1 or 2). Murphy testified he did not see anyone standing on Stemmons Freeway prior to, or after the motorcade passed.

Ed Hoffman maintains he did not see anyone as he stood and sat along the west shoulder of Stemmons Freeway. Officer Murphy testified he did not see anyone while he was assigned to his post on the east side of Stemmons Freeway. It is entirely possible both men were on the freeway at the same time but did not see each other due to the curvature of the roadway.

The center section of the bridge which crosses over Elm Street is approximately 15.5 feet at its highest point. The closest point from where Murphy testified he was standing, to the west side of Stemmons Freeway where Ed Hoffman maintains he stood, is approximately 75 yards measured on the diagonal. The height difference between these 2 points on the freeway is nearly 6 feet.

Photo 88 shows the curvature of Stemmons Freeway as it crosses over the top of Elm, Main and Commerce streets. If Officer Murphy was stationed on the freeway just over the crest of the roadway, and Ed was sitting down, and five lanes of vehicular traffic were passing between them, it is possible both men did not see each other. If Murphy had seen Hoffman, what could he have done about it? Would Murphy risk crossing 5 lanes of traffic to tell this citizen to get off the overpass?

Where was Officer Murphy?

Could Murphy have been at a different location prior to the arrival of the motorcade? Commission Document #205 is an interview of Officer Murphy by FBI agents Henry Oliver and Louis Kelley on December 9, 1963. The FBI field report suggests that Murphy *may* have been someplace other than his assigned post prior to the assassination:

> JOE MURPHY, Patrolman, Traffic Division, Police Department, Dallas, Texas, advised that on November 22, 1963, he was stationed on the triple overpass on Elm Street to assist in handling traffic. At approximately 10:30-10:40 AM, a pickup truck stalled on Elm Street between Houston Street and the underpass.

The Dallas police radio logs for channel 1, the police department's primary radio channel, recorded all radio traffic between the dispatchers, and the patrol officers. After the assassination, the police department was tasked with transcribing every radio conversation exchange that occurred that day. The transcripts were forwarded to the Warren Commission and entered into evidence as Commission Exhibit 705. The transcripts appear in Volume 17, from pages 361 to 494. In this exchange, Murphy calls in requesting a tow truck,

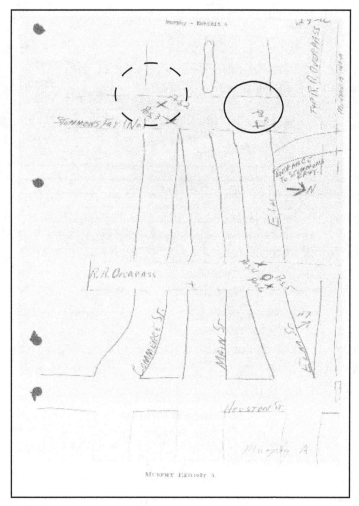

Photo 87: Murphy Exhibit A*

Officer Murphy located his position with an "X" and the letters "Pos. 1" (circle). During his testimony, Murphy was asked to locate where the other two officers were located on Stemmons Freeway. Murphy marked their positions with "X's" and the letters "Pos. 2" and "Pos. 3." (dashed line circle).

(Note the sketch locates the entrance ramp to Stemmons Freeway on the *east* side of Stemmons instead of the *west* side.)

*This exhibit will be used several more times to support other witnesses testimony.

Photo 88: This photo was taken from Ed Hoffman's location on the west side of Stemmons Freeway.

(DPD Officer Joe Murphy's radio number was 271)
271 (calling headquarters)
Dispatcher: 271
271: Could you send a city wrecker to the triple underpass; just west of the underpass on Elm to clear a stalled truck from the route of the escort?
Dispatcher: 10-4, 11:07.
271: Disregard the wrecker at the Triple Underpass. We got a truck to push him out of there.
Dispatcher: 10-4, 11:16.

The radio transcripts report Murphy calling for a wrecker at 11:07 a.m. At 11:16 a.m., Murphy calls in to headquarters and advises the dispatcher to disregard the tow truck. The FBI report states that Murphy deals with the stalled truck between 10:30 and 10:40 a.m. Why is there a discrepancy in the time? Did the agents misrepresent what Murphy told them?

If Murphy was on the triple overpass when he saw the stalled truck, which was on the *west* side of the triple overpass, he would have had to cross fourteen sets of railroad tracks, see the stalled truck, inquire from the "construction men" that the truck was disabled, cross the tracks again, and use the radio on his motorcycle to call the police dispatcher.

If Murphy was on *Stemmons Freeway* when he observed the "stalled truck," how was he able to determine the men in the truck needed assistance? Did he leave his post on the freeway, drive to the location where the truck was stopped, and then call for a tow truck?

The FBI report continues,

> There were three construction men in this truck, and he took one to the bank building to obtain another truck in order to assist in moving the stalled one.

Officer Murphy, by his own admission to the Warren Commission, was operating a three-wheeled motorcycle on the day of the assassination. He told the FBI he took one of the "construction men" back to the bank at Elm and Akard to obtain a second truck. Did this "construction man" ride on the back of Murphy's three-wheeler for nearly a mile? Did Murphy make this trip between 11:07 and 11:16?

In 1963, the Dallas police department did not have portable radios for their patrol officers. If an officer wanted to speak to the dispatcher, or to another officer, the only radios available were in their police cars or on their motorcycles. Murphy had to be near a police radio when he called about the stalled truck and again when he told the dispatcher to disregard the wrecker. Where did Murphy go after 11:16 a.m.?

Ed Hoffman's location was on the west side of Stemmons Freeway, above the Elm Street entrance ramp. Common sense suggests that Officer Murphy and any other officer assigned to control northbound traffic on Stemmons Freeway, would be parked on the east side of the highway, directly over the Elm, Main and Commerce underpass. If these officers stood on the west side of the freeway, they would *not* be able to see the approaching motorcade. According to the crude sketch Murphy drew for the Warren Commission (Murphy Exhibit A), he *was* on the east side of Stemmons Freeway, prior to the arrival of the motorcade.

In 1963, north and south-bound Stemmons Freeway was a five-lane highway with two non-driving lanes (shoulders) on either side. The standard width for vehicular traffic lanes is thirteen feet (13 feet x 5 driving lanes=65 feet). Adding one non-driving lane to each side gives a total width of approximately ninety-one (91) feet.

If Officer Murphy was standing on the *east* side of Stemmons Freeway, at a place where he could see the approaching motorcade, and Ed Hoffman was sitting on the railing on the *west* side directly above the entrance ramp with five lanes of vehicular traffic passing between them, is it entirely possible they simply *did not* or *could not* see each other.

Officer Murphy testified his assignment was to control northbound traffic on Stemmons Freeway, and stop it before the presidential motorcade arrived. The Mark Bell film shows northbound vehicular traffic moving on Stemmons Freeway, while the President's vehicle was traveling underneath the triple underpass. When did Murphy and the other officers stop northbound traffic? The motorcade was less than 100 yards from the entrance ramp. The vehicles on the highway should have already been stopped by this time.

Page 258 of "Case Closed," Posner continues, "But in addition to questions about whether Ed Hoffman was where he said he was that day, it appears that even if he was there, his view, 750 to 900 feet away, was blocked."

Is Posner referring to the distance between Ed Hoffman's location and the picket fence? We have already established this distance from the east end of the picket fence to Hoffman's position at 230 yards (690 feet). Again, why did Posner add an additional 70 yards (210 feet) to the total distance?

Posner's increase in the distance between Hoffman and the picket fence is deceptive. Is he suggesting this distance is too great for anyone to make out specific details, such as seeing man with a gun? A comparable distance of the distance between Hoffman's location to the east end of the picket fence is the same distance between the triple overpass and the intersection of Elm and Houston.

Posner writes that Hoffman's view "was blocked" but he does not specify what was "blocking" his view. If there was a vision obstruction, what was it?

Posner finishes this paragraph with, "Photographs and independent testimony reveal there were four large railway freight cars over the Elm Street tunnel that day, effectively obstructing any view from Stemmons into the rear of the grassy knoll."

Posner lists four different sources for this statement; the testimony of "Eugene Moore" from Volume 3, page 294; the testimony of Officer Earle Brown from Volume 6, page 233; and two interviews with Jim Moore. There is no listing for a "Eugene Moore" as a person who gave testimony before the Warren Commission. A closer examination of Posner's source of "Eugene Moore" is actually Dallas Deputy Sheriff, Eugene Boone.

Deputy Boone testified,

> **Mr. Cooper:** When you climbed over the retaining wall at the railroad yard, can you describe what the situation in the railroad yard was at that time? Were there railroad cars in the area?
>
> **Mr. Boone:** There were four railroad cars down approximately 100 yards from the retaining wall, right over the Elm Street tunnel, or portion of the triple underpass. Then there were some people down to the south of the triple underpass which had viewed the parade, or were viewing the parade I don't know. The city officer went back south, as I recall, and I went off to the north, northwest.

Photo 89: This aerial view of Dealey Plaza shows where Depuy Boone entered the railroad yards after climbing the retaining wall.

Photo 90: The arrow points to Dallas motorcycle officer Clyde Haygood on top of the retaining wall of the triple overpass. Deputy Boone, wearing a dark jacket, can be seen on the right side of Haygood.

Photo 91:This photo shows a clear view of the low wall connecting the top of the underpass to the wooden fence around the parking area in Dealey Plaza. (1991, Harry Yardum)

Deputy Boone's use of the words "down approximately 100 yards from the retaining wall" is vague and confusing. Which direction is "down?" The Warren Commission failed to ask Boone to clarify his use of the word "down." Boone testified he followed a Dallas motorcycle officer over "a little retaining wall that separates the freight yards there." Is Boone referring to where the bridge wall connects to the picket fence? The wall and the fence does separate the railroad yard from Dealey Plaza. Common sense, and historical photographs suggests this *has* to be where Boone climbed the wall (solid arrow on photo 89).

Deputy Boone likely followed Dallas motorcycle officer Clyde Haygood over the retaining wall. Officer Haygood can be seen standing on top of the retaining wall (photo 90). Deputy Boone then stated he observed "…four railroad cars 100 yards from the retaining wall, right over Elm Street tunnel." When Boone followed Haygood over this wall, the "four railroad cars" would have been ten to fifteen feet to his left in order for them to be over the Elm Street tunnel. It is unclear exactly where Boone is referring to in order to see four railroad cars 100 yards from the wall and still be over the Elm Street tunnel. Unfortunately the Warren Commission counsel did not attempt to clarify this statement and moved on to other matters.

Deputy Boone testified, "Then there were some people down to the south of the triple underpass which had viewed the parade…the city officer went back south as I recall, and I went off to the north, northwest."

South of the triple underpass? (white dotted box on photo 89). Is Boone describing the dozen railroad workers who were standing on the overpass? They weren't *south* of the triple underpass, they were *on* the triple overpass.

Boone testified, "The city officer went back south, as I recall, and I went off to the north, northwest." Why did Haygood go south away from the railroad yards? (white dashed line on photo 89). Why did Boone go north, northwest? (black dashed line on photo 89). Neither officer was asked why the went the directions they did after climbing the wall.

Officer Earle Brown

Posner's second source for the statement there were "four large railway freight cars over the Elm Street tunnel that day" was obtained from the Warren Commission testimony of Dallas police officer Earle Brown. Officer Brown and Officer Lomax were stationed on top of the railroad bridge over Stemmons Freeway. Only Brown was called to testify. He states,

> **Mr. Ball:** Did you see any people over in the railroad yards?
> **Mr. Brown:** Not that I recall; now they were moving trains in and out.
> **Mr. Ball:** But you did not see people standing?
> **Mr. Brown:** No, .sir; sure didn't.
> **Mr. Ball:** Everything was in clear view?
> **Mr. Brown:** Yes, sir.
> **Mr. Ball:** I withdraw the question. Was there any obstruction of your vision to the railroad yards?
> **Mr. Brown:** Yes.

Mr. Ball: What?

Mr. Brown: Not the direction of the railroad yard, but at ground level we didn't have very good view. Mr. Lomax and I remarked that we didn't have a very good view.

Mr. Ball: Was that because of the moving trains?

Mr. Brown: Yes, sir.

Officer Brown did not make *any* statement about "four large railway freight cars over the Elm Street tunnel." but does refer to the "moving trains." Where did Posner get his information? In addition, Brown did not volunteer any information about these "moving trains" nor was he asked to clarify exactly *where* he saw these "moving trains."

The "Cutty Sark" Billboard

Posner's book is loaded with elements of misinformation, inaccurate reporting, and false statements. On page 258, he writes, "Moreover, in 1963, a large Cutty Sark billboard also filled much of the space between the freeway and the railroad yards."

Posner cites Jim Moore as his source for this statement. Moore's information is wrong, which makes Posner's citation false. It is not known if Moore had seen the photographs of the billboard in Dealey Plaza taken by Mel McIntire before he spoke to Posner. The McIntire photos were taken as the limousine was leaving Dealey Plaza and clearly show the billboard's advertisement. We know Posner was familiar with at least one of the McIntire photos, because on page 259 of his book, he writes, "A photograph taken by Mel McIntire, snapped almost the precise moment…"

Both McIntire photos were taken from ground level looking east towards the triple underpass. In the background of both photos is a twenty-foot tall, thirty-foot long billboard advertising "Old Charter" bourbon. Posner even mistakes "Old Charter" with "Cutty Sark."

The Foliage

This last sentence Posner writes regarding Ed Hoffman is marked with an asterisk, which references a footnote at the bottom of page 258. He writes,

> The author drove to the location on Stemmons where Hoffman claimed to be on the day of the assassination. Even without the billboard and railroad cars, the foliage between the freeway and the railyard makes it difficult to see very much. Photographs show the foliage was as dense in 1963 as it is today. (Posner's book was published in 1993.)

Posner's source for this sentence was obtained from another conversation with Moore. Since Moore failed to mention Ed Hoffman in his book, "Conspiracy of One" (1990), why does Posner cite Moore's opinion on this matter as a source?

Assuming he visited Dealey Plaza some time before the book went to press, did he fail to consider the trees located between Stemmons Freeway and the railroad embankment would have continued to grow after 1963? His statement the foliage was as dense in 1963 as it was at the time he visited Dealey Plaza is a total fabrication of the facts. A simple examination of the photographs taken on the day of the assassination could have easily corrected this obvious error.

The only "foliage" visible in the Mel McIntire photographs (photos 50-51, page 65) and in photo 92 is a solitary bush/tree. This single tree is in the middle of an open landscape between the railroad yard and Stemmons Freeway. Is Posner referring to this tree as "dense foliage?" This single tree *was not* even in Ed Hoffman's line-of-sight. (There also appears to be a similar bush on the embankment behind the sign, out of Ed's line-of-sight).

The height of this leafless tree is between 10 and 12 feet tall. Ed Hoffman's location on Stemmons Freeway was a minimum of 15 feet above the Elm Street entrance ramp, the "Old Charter" billboard, and this tree. Both McIntire photos show that any "dense foliage" is in the background.

A number of Posner's statements are inaccurate and littered with false documentation. By 1993, (when "Case Closed" was published), there were hundreds of books on the Kennedy assassination, many containing photographs of Dealey Plaza at the time of the shooting. Gerald Posner failed to accurately research this case and distorted the truth for profit. Shame on you Mr. Posner.

Photo 92: This photo taken after 1966 shows the area between the triple underpass and Stemmons Freeway. The arrow points to the tree/bush in the area the Freeway and the railroad yards. When this picture was taken, there were no trees blocking Ed Hoffman's view into the parking area behind the picket fence.

Vincent Bugliosi "Reclaiming History"

The opening line of Vincent Bugliosi's book, "Reclaiming History" (2007),

> Although there have been hundreds of books on the JFK assassination, no book has even attempted to be a comprehensive and fair evaluation of the entire case, including all of the major conspiracy theories.

In this 1400 page rehash of the "lone nut assassin," Bugliosi spends the majority of his effort criticizing those who dispute the government's conclusions. He writes, "Conspiracy theorists have wrought a grave injustice on the [Warren] Commission and performed a flagrant disservice to the American public."

The subtitle for this section of his book is entitled "The Zanies." In it, Bugliosi spends only one and one-third page on the observations of Ed Hoffman (pages 873-874). His classification of those who disagree with the "official findings" are in his words, "Gestating for decades in the nation's marrow which obviously has to have had a deleterious effect on the way American's view those who lead them and determine their destiny."

He writes that "Ed was deaf at birth," which is incorrect. Ed lost his hearing about the time he turned 4 years old. He claims Ed receives payment for his autograph, which is not true, and Bugliosi provides no proof otherwise. Ed Hoffman has made countless appearances in public related to the assassination of President Kennedy: The Assassination Symposium on Kennedy (ASK), the JFK Lancer International Conferences and Student Symposia, and the Coalition on Political Assassinations (COPA). Ed Hoffman has *never* charged money for autographs or photographs.

In the remainder of this section, Bugliosi summarizes the 1967 FBI report filed by Agent Griffin. Bugliosi spends considerable time and energy trying to convince the reader that those witnesses who observed things that did not conform to the "lone assassin in the building" scenario as "cuckoo birds" or "crackpots." He uses the terms, "bizarre observations," "silly stories," "lacks credibility," "far-fetched" and "fantastic."

Vincent Bugliosi compares Ed Hoffman's account of the activity behind the picket fence to the "Elvis is still alive" syndrome. A good case for slander could be made about his final statement about Ed Hoffman. He writes on page 874,

> The conspiracy theorists are so impoverished in their desperate search for evidence to support their cause they are compelled to descend to such whimsical ever-changing and obviously untrue accounts as that of Virgil Hoffman.

Mr. Bugliosi's deliberate misrepresentation of the facts is an insult to those who are honesty researching this case in an effort to learn the truth. Shame on you, Mr. Bugliosi.

Another Brick in the Wall

"Frankly I thought they [shots] were coming from right over by the fence...they sounded if they were coming from right in there."

JEAN HILL

Suspicious activity behind the picket fence

Lee Bowers was the railroad switchman for the Union Terminal Company at the time of the assassination. Of all the witnesses in and around Dealey Plaza that day, Bowers had the best view of the parking lot on the west side of the book depository, including the backside of the picket fence. From his elevated position inside the switching tower, Bowers was able to observe vehicles and people coming into and leaving the parking lot below him.

Minutes after the assassination, Bowers was contacted by Dallas County Deputy Sheriff Eugene Boone who was searching the parking lot and railroad yards. Later that same day, Bowers arrived at the sheriff's office and gave a hand-written statement of what he had observed. Bowers then waited at the sheriff's office while his hand-written statement was typed onto an affidavit. The information on the affidavit is taken directly from the hand-written statement:

> I was on duty today and about 11:55 am I saw a dirty 1959 Oldsmobile Station Wagon come down the street toward my Building. This street dead ends in the railroad yard…This car just drove around slowly and left the area.

Sometime later that afternoon, Bowers was interviewed by FBI agents Robert Barrett and John Almon. The FBI report filed by these agents is very similar to the information Bowers provided in his hand-written statement. However, Barrett and Almon added some additional information:

> He [Bowers] saw no one run from the west or south sides of the Texas School Book Depository Building and prior to the shooting did not see any suspicious person enter the building.

At the time of the shooting, Bowers saw two strangers near the picket fence — one man was middle aged and heavy set, the other appeared to be in his mid-twenties wearing a plaid shirt. Bowers recognized everyone else he saw in the area as railroad employees except these two men.

When Bowers testified to the Warren Commission, he was questioned by assistant counsel Joseph Ball. Bowers testified,

> **Mr. Ball:** Now, were there people standing on the high side — high ground between your tower and where Elm Street goes down under the underpass toward the mouth of the underpass?
> **Mr. Bowers:** Directly in line, towards the mouth of the underpass, there were two men. One man, middle-aged, or slightly older, fairly heavy-set, in a white shirt, fairly dark trousers. Another younger man, about mid-twenties, in either a plaid shirt or plaid coat or jacket. They were looking up towards Main and Houston and following the caravan as it came down. One of them was middle-aged, heavyset. Each of 'em had uniforms. (Volume 6, p. 286)

On October 1, 2001, JFK assassination researcher Debra Conway interviewed Olan Degaugh, who was the Supervisor of the Yard Department with the Union Terminal Railroad Company and was directly over Lee Bowers' boss, Sam "Skinny" Holland. Conway provided the authors with the notes from that interview,

> At the time of the assassination, along with his railroad job, Degaugh owned D's Parking, which started where the Hyatt Regency Hotel is now and went around the railroad tower behind the Texas School Book Depository.

> Degaugh had a conversation with Lee Bowers sometime after the assassination and learned that from his location inside the switching tower, Bowers saw a man open the trunk of this car and put something inside and then the vehicle left the area. The car, an older coupe of some kind, an older car, was parked next to the picket fence.

> Although Degaugh claimed Bowers never said why he didn't tell everything he saw before he died. Degaugh felt Bowers never told the authorities about the men, the car, or what he saw these men doing immediately after the shooting because he did not want to be more involved in the assassination controversy. Degaugh said that Bowers was a good worker and a fine person. Further, Degaugh described Bowers as all business, didn't talk very much and while he was somewhat of an introvert. was very credible.

On September 8, 2003, Conway conducted a second interview of Olan Degaugh who provided this additional information,

> He [Degaugh] quoted Sam Holland telling him that the shots sounded like popcorn being popped. Standing on the railroad bridge he [Holland] believed the sounds were coming from the north or east side of the fence line.

> Degaugh said that Bowers told him that he saw someone running away. This person put something inside a car, get into the car and drive away. Degaugh said that Bowers told him it looked like a rifle.

The Rambler Station Wagon

In this section, the focus will be on four witnesses who independently corroborate Ed Hoffman's statement regarding a Rambler station in the area of Dealey Plaza. Ed observed a green Rambler station wagon enter the parking lot on the west side of the book depository. This vehicle drove into the lot via the Elm Street annex. He watched this vehicle for just a few moments believing at the time that the driver was simply looking for a parking space. Ed said he saw this vehicle finally park near the northwest side of the railroad switching tower.

After the armed confrontation between the man in the business suit and the uniformed police officer (later identified as Joe Marshall Smith) the man in the business suit walked over to the Rambler station wagon and get in on the passenger side. Hoffman communicated the vehicle went north along the north side of the parking lot and turned right onto Houston Street. This was the last time Hoffman saw this vehicle.

Richard Carr and the Rambler

Richard Randolph Carr watched the motorcade pass through Dealey Plaza from a position on top of an outdoor scaffold six stories above the roadway at the Criminal Courts building. During his January 4, 1964 interview with the FBI, Carr said from his elevated position, he could see directly into the windows on the 6th floor of the book depository. Carr told the FBI he saw a heavy-set man wearing a hat, a tan sport coat and horn-rimmed glasses on the 6th floor of the Texas School Book Depository at the southeast corner window.

On February 3, 1964, Carr was interviewed a second time by FBI agent Paul Scott. Agent Scott's interview was submitted to the Warren Commission and marked Commission Document 385. On page 2 of Carr's statement, he states,

> When I reached the ground I walked to Houston St. and down Houston St. to the Commerce St. intersection…While I was on Houston St. near the Commerce St. intersection I saw a man whom I believe was identical with the man I had earlier seen looking out of the window of the Texas School Book Depository building. This man, walking very fast, proceeded on Houston St. south to Commerce St., then east on Commerce St. to Record St., which is one block from Houston St. This man got into a 1961 or 1962 Grey Rambler Station Wagon which was parked just north of Commerce on Record St. The station wagon, which had Texas license and was driven by a young Negro man, drove off in a northerly direction.

Richard Carr was not called as a witness before the Warren Commission. He received death threats over the telephone, ordering him to leave Texas and he eventually moved to Montana.

Deputy Sheriff Roger Craig and the Rambler station wagon

Roger Craig was a deputy sheriff for Dallas County at the time of the assassination. Craig's law enforcement career was distinguished until November 22, 1963.

He had received numerous honors for his work and dedication to the county and citizens of Dallas. It wasn't until after his testimony concerning what he saw on the day of the assassination that his law enforcement career deteriorated. Eventually he was forced off the sheriff's department and prevented from working in law enforcement. Craig told assassination researcher Penn Jones he believed that his former employer, Dallas County Sheriff Bill Decker was responsible for "black-balling" him from police work.

On the day of the assassination, Craig was standing on the Main Street steps of the Dallas County Courthouse along with several other members of the sheriff's department. Deputy Craig saw the President pass by his location and watched as the motorcade turned left onto Houston Street. When Craig heard the first rifle shot, he immediately jumped off the steps and ran west on Main towards Houston Street. Just as he approached the corner,

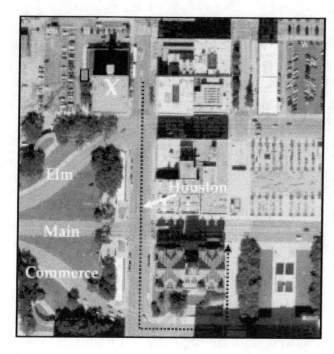

Photo 93: This aerial view traces the path of the man Carr saw in the 6th floor window of the book depository. The book depository is designated with the letter X as the starting point for the man seen by Carr.

two more rifle shots rang out. Craig then ran full speed towards Elm Street and noticed people lying on the ground in the plaza. A Dallas police officer was running up the grassy knoll towards the picket fence. Craig followed this officer.

When Craig got behind the picket fence, he questioned several witnesses who told him that they thought the shots had come from behind the picket fence. Deputy Craig spoke to Arnold Rowland and after hearing what he had observed, started to walk him over the Sheriff's office for further questioning when he saw Dallas County Deputy Lewis in the area. Craig handed Rowland over to Lewis and directed him to escort him to the sheriff's office to fill out a witness statement.

At about 12:40, Craig was standing with dozens of witnesses on the north side of Elm Street. Craig said he heard someone whistle and saw a white male in his twenties run down the grassy knoll from the direction of the book depository. This individual entered a green Rambler station wagon that had a luggage rack attached to the top. This vehicle pulled to the north curb and the running man got into the car. Craig described the man driving the vehicle as Latin-looking, husky, dark wavy hair, wearing a tan windbreaker-type jacket.

Craig said he tried to step across Elm and was going to stop this vehicle but because traffic was so heavy, he was unable to cross safely. Deputy Craig made his way over to the front of the book depository and tried to find someone who might be in charge so that he could report what he had just observed. While he stood in front of the building, Craig said he made contact with a white male, about 40 years of age, with sandy hair and a cleft chin dressed in a gray suit. According to Craig, this man identified himself as a Secret Service agent who listened to Craig's story and the only thing he seemed interested in was the description of the Rambler.

Later that afternoon, when Craig heard about the arrest of Oswald, he called Captain Will Fritz and told him about the incident with the Rambler station wagon, and of seeing a man running from the direction of the book depository. Fritz told Craig to come to the police station to see if the person they had in custody was the same man he saw leaving the area.

At 4:30 p.m., Craig arrived at police headquarters and saw Oswald sitting in the Homicide Office. He immediately identified Oswald as the same individual he saw leaving in the Rambler. Craig recalled that this exchange took place between Fritz and Oswald while he was present,

> **Fritz:** This man (pointing to Craig) saw you leave.
> **Oswald:** I told you I did.
> **Fritz:** Take it easy son, we're just trying to find out what happened. What about the car?
> **Oswald:** That station wagon belongs to Mrs. Paine. Don't try to drag her into this. Everybody will know who I am now.

What is interesting in this exchange between Captain Fritz and Oswald is his response to Fritz's statement about a "car" prompted him to specifically call it a "station wagon." How did Oswald know that they were referring to a station wagon? Ruth Paine did own a station wagon with luggage rack on top but according to the police, it was not a Nash Rambler.

On November 23, 1963, Craig submitted a Supplementary Investigation Report to Sheriff Bill Decker. In that report, Craig writes;

> About this time I heard a shrill whistle and I turned around and saw a white male running down the hill from the direction of the Texas School Book Depository Building and I saw what I think was a light colored Rambler Station wagon with luggage rack on top pull over to the curb and this subject who had come running down the hill get into this car. The man driving this station wagon was a dark complected white male.

That same day, Craig was interviewed by Special Agent James Bookhout who submitted a report identical to what Craig wrote in his Supplementary Report. However, Bookhout's report has Craig describing the Rambler as "white" and the driver as "a Negro male."

On November 25, 1963, Craig was interviewed a second time by the FBI. Special Agent Benjamin Keutzer wrote a report nearly identical to the report filed by Bookhout. Agent Keutzer's report was submitted to the Warren Commission and designated Commission Exhibit 1932. In this report, Keutzer states that the vehicle seen by Craig was "white" in color. The next paragraph has Craig stating,

> Mr. CRAIG described the driver of the automobile as a white male, American, dark-complected, short hair, wearing a light colored jacket. Mr. CRAIG stated he had previously described this man as a Negro male, but has since decided that the driver was a white male.

It is also interesting to note the difference between the information Craig provided in his report to the Dallas Sheriff and the information contained in the first and second FBI

Photo 94: This photo, taken by Jim Murray, shows a light-colored station wagon traveling west on Elm Street (arrow). Deputy Roger Craig said this vehicle pulled to the curb and a white male resembling Lee Oswald ran down the incline and got in on the passenger side.

Photo 95: This is a cropped version of photo 97 shows the station wagon seen by Deputy Craig traveling west on Elm.

reports. Craig's written report states the vehicle was "light colored" and both FBI reports say the vehicle was "white."

In April 1964, Craig appeared before Warren Commission Counsel David Belin in Dallas. When Craig entered the interview room he noticed a tape recorder and a female holding a legal pad. Belin did not start the tape recorder and instructed the young woman with the notepad only to take notes when she was directed to do so by Belin. Deputy Craig's account of the first few minutes of the session was more of a "pre-interview." Finally the tape recorder was turned on and the woman began taking notes. After a few preliminary questions, Belin turned the recorder off and told the woman to stop taking notes. Craig said later that any time Belin didn't want the testimony recorded; he would turn off the machine. At the conclusion of the interview, Craig was not given the opportunity to sign his statement and was simply told to leave.

Craig told JFK assassination researcher Penn Jones that when he first had the opportunity to read his Warren Commission testimony as it appeared in the 26 volumes, he was shocked to discover that his account was changed in at least fifteen different places.

He gave Penn Jones a listing of the discrepancies between what he told the authorities and what was printed in the Warren Commission regarding his story about the Rambler station wagon:

- He told David Belin that the Rambler was "light green" but in the printed testimony, the color is "white."

- He told Belin that the driver of this vehicle was wearing a tan jacket, but in the printed testimony the jacket was "white."

- Craig said the license plate on the Rambler was *not the* same color as a Texas license plate, but in the printed testimony the word "not" was omitted so that it appeared that the license plate *was* the same color as a Texas plate.

- He told Belin that he got a good look at the driver of the Rambler, but the printed testimony was changed to "Craig did not get a good look at the driver of this vehicle."

To fully appreciate Deputy Craig's sworn testimony as it appears in the Warren Commission, the reader is encouraged to read the entire exchange between Craig and David Belin in Volume 6, on pages 260-273. The following is a portion of Craig's testimony regarding the Rambler station wagon:

> **Mr. Craig:** No; we didn't find anything at that time. Now, as we were searching, we had just got over across the street, when I heard someone whistle.
> **Mr. Belin:** Now, about how many minutes was this after the time that you had turned that young couple over to Lemmy Lewis that you heard this whistle?
> **Mr. Craig:** Fourteen or 15 minutes.
> **Mr. Belin:** Fourteen or 15 minutes?
> **Mr. Craig:** Yes.
> **Mr. Belin:** Was this, you mean, after the shooting?
> **Mr. Craig:** After the—from the time I heard the first shot.

Mr. Belin: All right. Your heard someone whistle?

Mr. Craig: Yes. So I turned and—uh-saw a man start to run down the hill on the north side of Elm Street, running down toward Elm Street.

Mr. Belin: And, about where was he with relation to the School Book Depository Building?

Mr. Craig: Uh—directly across that little side street that runs in front of it, He was on the south side of it.

Mr. Belin: And he was on the south side of what would be an Extension of Elm Street, if Elm Street didn't curve down into the underpass?

Mr. Craig: Eight; right,

Mr. Belin: And where was he with relation to the west side of the School Book Depository Building?

Mr. Craig: Right by the—uh—well, actually, directly in line with the west corner—the southwest corner,

Mr. Belin: He was directly in line with the southwest corner of the building?

Mr. Craig: Yes.

Mr. Belin: And he was on the south curve of that street that runs right in front of the building there?

Mr. Craig: Yes.

Mr. Belin: And he started to run toward Elm Street as it curves under the underpass?

Mr. Craig: Yes, directly down the grassy portion of the park.

Mr. Belin: All right. And then what did you see happen?

Mr. Craig: I saw a light-colored station wagon, driving real slow, coming west on Elm Street from Houston. Uh— actually, it was nearly in line with him. And the driver was leaning to his right looking up the hill at the man running down.

Mr. Belin: Uh-huh.

Mr. Craig: And the station wagon stopped almost directlyacross from me. And—uh—the man continued down the hill and got in the station wagon. And I attempted to cross the street. I wanted to talk to both of them. But the—uh—traffic was so heavy I couldn't get across the street. And—uh—they were gone before I could...

Mr. Belin: Where did the station wagon head?

Mr. Craig: West on Elm Street.

Mr. Belin: Under the triple underpass?

Mr. Craig: Yes.

Mr. Belin: Could you describe the man that you saw running down toward the station wagon?

Mr. Craig: Oh, he was a white male in his twenties, five nine, five eight, something like that; about 140 to 150; had kind of medium brown sandy hair—you know, it was like it'd been blown—you know, he'd been in the wind or something—it was all wild-looking; had on—uh—blue trousers--

Mr. Belin: What shade of blue? Dark blue, medium or light?

Mr. Craig: No; medium, probably; I'd say medium. And, a—uh—light tan shirt, as I remember it.

Mr. Belin: Anything else about him?

Mr. Craig: No; nothing except that he looked like he was in an awful hurry.

Mr. Belin: What about the man who was driving the car?

Mr. Craig: Now, he struck me, at first, as being a colored male. He was very dark complected, had real dark short hair, and was wearing a thin white-looking Jacket—uh, it looked like the short windbreaker type, you know, because it was real thin and had the collar that came out over the shoulder (indicating with hands) like that—just a short jacket.

Mr. Belin: You say that he first struck you that way. Do you now think that he was a Negro?

Mr. Craig: Well, I don't—I didn't get a real good look at him. But my first glance at him—I was more interested in the man coming down the hill—but my first glance at him, he struck me as a Negro.

Mr. Belin: Is that what your opinion is today?

Mr. Craig: Well, I—I couldn't say, because I didn't get a good enough look.

Mr. Belin: What kind and what color station wagon was it?

Mr. Craig: It was light colored—almost—uh—it looked white to me.

Mr. Belin: What model or make was it?

Mr. Craig: I thought it was a Nash.

Mr. Belin: Why would you think it was a Nash?

Mr. Craig: Because it had a built-in luggage rack on 'the top. And—uh—at the time, this was the only type car I could fit with that type luggage rack.

Mr. Belin: A Nash Rambler-is that what you're referring to?

Mr. Craig: Yes; with a rack on the back portion of the car, you know.

Mr. Belin: Did it have a Texas license plate, or not?

Mr. Craig: It had the same color. I couldn't see the—uh—name with the numbers on it. I could just barely make them out. They were at an angle where I couldn't make the numbers of the—uh—any of the writing on it. But—uh—I'm sure it was a Texas plate.

Mr. Belin: Anything else about this incident that you can recall?

Mr. Craig. No; not that...

Mr. Belin: All right. Then what did you do?

(Volume 6, pgs. 266-267)

Deputy Craig's assertions appear in three different documents were published in the Warren Commission documents, two of them dated November 23, 1963, and the third dated November 25, 1963. Each document specifically mentions a Rambler, although the published testimony does not.

Deputy Craig said his references to a Rambler were changed to "station wagon."

According to the Warren Commission, Lee Oswald fled the area minutes after the shooting, first by bus, then by taxicab, which took him to within blocks of his rooming house in Oak Cliff. Page 160 of the Warren Report states, "…The Commission could not accept important elements of Craig's testimony…and that while Craig may have seen someone fleeing, this man was not Lee Harvey Oswald."

Months before Craig's death in 1975, assassination researcher Penn Jones published two of his letters in the newsletter, "The Continuing Inquiry." Craig discussed his testimony with Warren Commission Counsel David Belin,

> As for what was on the tape of my testimony that is missing, Berlin [Belin] asked me to identify some clothing which I did and this is all changed. However it was

correct on the tape also the description of the suspect and the station wagon were correct on the tape but not in my testimony.

Marvin Robinson and the Rambler station wagon

On November 23, 1963, FBI agents John Almon and J. Calvin Rice, interviewed Marvin C. Robinson regarding his observations the previous day. The report filed by these agents was submitted to the Warren Commission and marked Commission Document 5. Mr. Robinson was not called before the Warren Commission. The first paragraph of the agent's report states,

> MARVIN C. ROBINSON, [address and phone number omitted here] advised that approximately between 12:30 and 1:00 p.m. on the afternoon of November 22, 1963, while traveling west on Elm Street he crossed the intersection of Elm and Houston Streets shortly after the assassination of President KENNEDY. ROBINSON stated that after he had crossed Houston Street and was in front of the Texas School Book Depository building a light colored Nash stationwagon suddenly appeared before him. He stated this vehicle stopped and a white male came down the grass covered incline between the building and the street and entered the stationwagon after which it drove away in the direction of the Oak Cliff section of Dallas. ROBINSON stated he does not recall the license number of the stationwagon or whether or not it bore a Texas license plate.

Roy Cooper and the Rambler station wagon

Assassination researcher Chris Courtwright discovered an FBI interview of another witness by the name of Roy Cooper who encountered a Rambler station wagon in Dealey Plaza. This document provides additional corroboration for Ed Hoffman, Richard Carr, Roger Craig, and Marvin Robinson regarding this vehicle. Cooper was interviewed FBI Special Agent Earle Haley. Agent Haley's report states,

> Mr. Roy Cooper, Route 1, Box 135A, Euless, Texas, phone Butler 3-2640, furnished the following information at 12:15 p.m. this date [ll-23-63]. He related an incident about a Nash Rambler being seen leaving the building at Elm and Houston on 11/22/63. He was driving his car and following his boss who was driving a Cadillac. They were coming south on Houston and had to wait for the parade and the incident happened shortly after they reached this intersection. Cooper observed a white male somewhere between 20 and 30 years of age wave at a Nash Rambler station wagon, light colored, as it pulled out and was ready to leave from Elm and Houston. This station wagon pulled out real fast in front of the Cadillac driven by his boss and his employer had to stop abruptly and nearly hit this Nash Rambler. Cooper could not see who was driving the Nash Rambler and could not furnish any further description of the man who jumped into this car. They drove off at a rather fast rate of speed and went down toward the overpass toward Oak Cliff.

Cooper was following his supervisor Marvin C. Robinson who was taking his Cadillac home to Oak Cliff. Cooper was then to pick up Robinson and they were to go back to their place of employment in Garland in his car. Cooper and Robinson are both employed at Ling Temco Vought at Garland, Texas. He believed that Robinson could give further information about the Rambler station wagon, also the driver and the rider.

What is intriguing about this pattern of evidence is the way in which the details interlock. None of these witnesses could have known of the other reports filed by Carr and Craig. Richard Carr's description of the station wagon and its driver dovetails perfectly with the description supplied by Robinson, Cooper and Craig.

This vehicle was headed in a northerly direction when Carr saw it on Record Street—two blocks north, a left turn and it would be headed west on Elm Street and would pass in front of the book depository (photo 93).

Movements of the Rambler station wagon

This vehicle was first seen by Ed Hoffman as it drove into the parking lot via the Elm Street access road. The vehicle drove around the lot, and according to Ed, appeared to be looking for a parking spot;

Lee Bowers observed a station wagon drive into the parking lot at about 11:55 a.m. Bowers said that this vehicle drove slowly around the lot. He thought the vehicle left the area.

Immediately after the shooting, Ed watched the man in the business suit walk over to this Rambler and get in on the passenger side. Ed saw this vehicle drive along the north side of the book depository and turn right onto Houston Street.

Richard Carr saw a man in a tan jacket walking south on Houston Street and turn the corner onto Commerce Street and get into a light colored Rambler station wagon which was parked on Record Street. Carr saw this vehicle drive north on Record Street towards Elm.

Marvin Robinson was driving through the intersection of Elm and Houston when he saw a Rambler station wagon traveling west on Elm Street in front of him. Robinson watched as a white male came running down the grassy incline between the book depository and the street. This male subject entered the station wagon and watched as it continued towards the triple overpass.

While standing along the north curb of Elm Street, Deputy Sheriff Roger Craig saw a white male running down the hill from the direction of the book depository and get into a light colored Rambler station wagon.

Were Hoffman and Bowers describing the same station wagon? Recall that Bowers specifically mentioned in his affidavit to the Sheriff's office he saw a black Oldsmobile station wagon driving around in the parking lot. Ed said the only station wagon he saw driving around in the parking lot was a light colored Rambler. It is entirely possible that these two men saw two different vehicles.

The vehicle seen by these five witnesses was specifically identified as a Rambler station wagon. Did these five witnesses conspire to tell the same story about seeing a light-colored Rambler station wagon in Dealey Plaza before and immediately after the shooting?

The evidence is overwhelming these five individuals saw the same Rambler station wagon driving in and around Dealey Plaza minutes after the shooting. The odds of these five witnesses seeing five different Rambler station wagons within two blocks of Dealey Plaza minutes after the shooting would be astronomical.

The mystery surrounding the green/white/light-colored, Oldsmobile or Nash Rambler station wagon may never be solved. The license plate was not observed by any witnesses; the driver was never identified; and the vehicle's owner at the time of the assassination can not be established beyond a reasonable doubt. What is consistent are the statements of four independent witnesses who recall seeing an identical vehicle within a four block radius of the Texas School Book Depository before and moments after the shooting of President Kennedy.

- One witness saw a man fire a rifle in the direction of President Kennedy's vehicle from behind the picket fence. That same man was seen entering a Rambler station wagon moments after the shooting. The vehicle drove out of the area and made a right turn onto Houston.

- Another witness saw this vehicle drive south on Houston from the book depository, and turn left onto Commerce Street. This same witness saw the vehicle turn off of Commerce onto Record Street and park. This witness then observed a man running south on Houston, turn the corner on Commerce and turn again at Record Street. This running man then entered the Rambler station wagon. The vehicle then proceeded north on Record Street towards Elm.

- A third witness saw a Rambler station wagon traveling west on Elm just past Houston Street. This witness said the vehicle stopped at the curb on Elm and a white male ran and got in and the vehicle drove towards the triple overpass.

- The last witness saw a Rambler station wagon stop at the curb on Elm and watched as a white male ran down the grass incline and enter the vehicle on the passenger side.

When a witness is called to testify about an event, juries may decide not to believe the witness for a variety of reasons. If their recollection is not persuasive enough, reasonable doubt may exist. If a second witness gives testimony about seeing the same event, juries might be prone to give that testimony more probative value. Add two more witnesses who testify that they saw the same event in similar detail; a defense attorney would probably be willing to concede that reasonable doubt no longer exists.

The observations of these four independent witnesses regarding a Rambler station wagon at different points in Dealey Plaza can no longer be considered a coincidence. A solid case could be made that these four people saw the same vehicle in Dealey Plaza moments after the shooting!

Any number of scenarios can be imagined regarding the story behind this Rambler station wagon — the vehicle was purchased by the conspirators using false or real names; it was stolen from the true owner; the license plate was stolen from a vehicle registered in Texas, the vehicle actually belonged to the driver who was told to be at a certain location to pick up and deliver the passengers to a specific location. One rational explanation might be that this vehicle was used to transport the shooter/s to various locations in and around Dealey Plaza and after the shooting, was used as getaway vehicle. This last option makes the most sense based on the evidence presented.

Assassination researcher Richard Bartholomew did an extensive study of this vehicle and its mysterious connections to the assassination. In his manuscript, "Possible Discovery of an Automobile Used in the JFK Conspiracy," (1993) Bartholomew discusses the various links between the assassination and the Rambler, and traces those relationships to names that have become familiar with assassination researchers.

In May 1989, Bartholomew found an identical Rambler on the campus of the University of Texas in Austin. Bartholomew found apparent associations between it and persons whose lives were intertwined with Lyndon Johnson's political machine, the military-industrial-intelligence complex, right-wing politics, and Latin American politics.

In November 1990, Bartholomew paid two dollars and obtained the ownership history for this vehicle. It was hoped that the records would show the vehicle would have belonged to Ruth and Michael Paine. Unfortunately, ownership records prior to title numbers beginning with the digits "85" were routinely destroyed, which included those for this vehicle. Fortunately the same man had owned the car since 1963. The current owner of this 1959 Rambler Cross County Custom station wagon, Texas license 711-TQC was "George Gordon Wing" of Austin, Texas. The vehicle's previous owner was "CE Smith Motors, Austin, Texas."

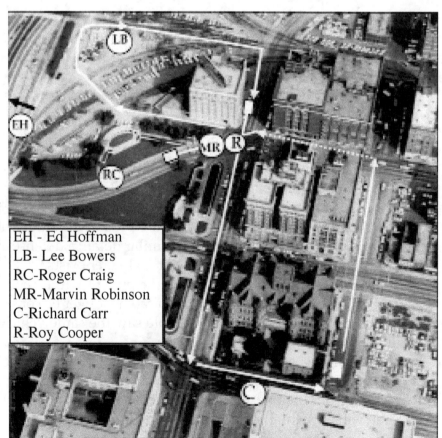

Photo 96: This aerial view of Dealey Plaza shows the route of the Rambler station wagon seen by seven witnesses between 12:31 and 12:40 p.m.

EH - Ed Hoffman
LB- Lee Bowers
RC-Roger Craig
MR-Marvin Robinson
C-Richard Carr
R-Roy Cooper

Bartholomew writes,

> The possibility remains that the Paines owned the car prior to "C.E. Smith"
> because its ownership history during the final four years is yet to be established
> despite several attempts through various means. But just because Oswald was
> under the impression that the car belonged to Ruth Paine in 1963 does not mean
> that it did.

SAM HOLLAND

Except for Lee Bowers, the witnesses with the best view of the fenced-in area were those standing above Elm Street on the triple overpass. As the motorcade approached, 13 railroad employees and two Dallas police officers were on the overpass, the grassy knoll and the picket fence was just to their left. Not one of the railroad employees were called before the Warren Commission, and only four were questioned by counsel for the Commission. Nine of them were questioned by agents of the FBI. The first interview took place almost four months after the assassination on March 17, 1964. The FBI did not give verbatim transcripts of these interviews to the Commission, but provided only summaries of the interviews. In addition, not one FBI agent who interviewed any witness in this case ever appeared before the Commission to give testimony of what the witness told them.

Five of these men said that shots came from the knoll and six others said that when the shots were fired their attention was immediately attracted towards the knoll. Of those present in Dealey Plaza during the shooting, those on top of the overpass were in a unique position to observe smoke coming from behind the fence. Seven railroad employees said they did see smoke above the bushes and under the trees immediately after hearing the shots.

One of these men was Sam Holland, Signal Supervisor for the Union Terminal Railroad. On November 22, 1963, Holland stood on the overpass directly in front of Officer Foster and watched the motorcade along with several of his employees. After the assassination, Holland went to the sheriff's office and submitted an affidavit in which he stated,

> I am signal supervisor for the Union Terminal and I was inspecting signal and
> switches and stopped to watch the parade. I was standing on top of the triple
> underpass and the President's car was coming down Elm Street and when they
> got just about to the Arcade I heard what I thought for the moment was a fire
> cracker and he [JFK] slumped over and I looked over toward the arcade and
> trees and saw a puff of smoke come from the trees and I heard three more shots
> after the first shot but that was the only puff of smoke I saw. I immediately ran
> around to where I could see behind the arcade and did not see anyone running
> from there. But the puff of smoke I saw definitely came from behind the arcade
> through the trees. After the first shot the President slumped over and Mrs.
> Kennedy jumped up and tried to get over the back seat to him and then the
> second shot rang out. After the first shot the secret service man raised up in the
> seat with a machine gun and then dropped back down in the seat. And they
> immediately sped off. Everything is spinning in my head and if I remember
> anything else later I will come back and tell Bill [Sheriff Decker].

The next paragraph of the FBI report states,

> …and saw Governor CONNALLY, sitting directly in front of the President fall forward and at the same time, Governor CONNALLY's wife knelt down behind the Governor's fallen body on the floor of the car.

Paragraph three of the FBI report states,

> When the first shot was fired, HOLLAND stated that a motorcycle officer behind the car stopped his motor, left it in the street, drew his gun, and began running back toward the intersection of Elm and Houston Street. One of the officers in the front seat of the Presidential car stood up with a machine gun in his hands and was looking back from the car when it immediately speeded up, throwing this officer back across the front seat.

From Holland's statement, we assume he is describing the actions of Dallas police officer Bobby Hargis, who was riding at the left rear of the limousine during the motorcade. Immediately after the shooting, Hargis parked his motorcycle against the south curb of Elm and ran directly to where the picket fence and the overpass wall meet. From Hargis' own Warren Commission testimony he told Assistant Counsel Stern.

> **Stern:** All right, what did you do then? You say you parked your motorcycle
> **Hargis:** Yes, uh-huh—
> **Stern:** Where?
> **Hargis:** It was to the left-hand side of the street from—south side of Elm Street.
> **Stern:** And then what did you do?
> **Hargis:** I ran across the street looking over towards the railroad overpass and I remembered seeing people scattering and running and then I looked...
> **Stern:** People on the overpass?

Where did the agents get the information that Hargis ran towards Elm and Houston? If they didn't get it from Hargis' testimony, did they misunderstand what Holland said, or did they purposely misrepresent what Holland told them?

This is not the first incident where information contained within an FBI report has been questioned by the very person who was the subject of the interview.

The last paragraph of the FBI report states,

> HOLLAND stated that he looked toward the fence to his left to observe anyone that he might see running from this fence but saw no one. The only unusual thing that HOLLAND could recall was an approximate one and one-half to two foot diameter of what he believed was gray smoke which appeared to him to be coming from the trees which would have been on the right of the Presidential car but observed no one there or in the vicinity.

Here the FBI acknowledges the presence of smoke on the knoll immediately after the shooting. If they would have interviewed the other 13 people who stood on the overpass, they might have been confronted with the fact that the majority of them saw smoke as well.

On April 8, 1964, Sam Holland appeared before Warren Commission counsel Samuel Stern. Holland had retained Dallas attorney Balford Morrison to represent him during his appearance before the government. During his testimony, Holland tells Stern about the people on the overpass,

> **Stern:** And these policemen that you spoke to, there were 3 altogether?
> **Holland:** Two—there were 2 city policemen and 1 man in plainclothes. I didn't talk to him. I talked to the city policemen.
> **Stern:** You don't know what his affiliation was?
> **Holland:** I know he was a plainclothes detective, or FBI agent, or something.

Who was this "plainclothes" person? If it was a detective, it wasn't anyone from the Dallas police department. According to the duty assignment sheets prepared by Assistant Chief Bachelor, only two uniformed officers were assigned to the triple overpass, Foster and White. If it was an FBI agent, there is no record of his assignment there. Holland had worked for the railroad for twenty-five years and testified he "…knew all the workers, except for one or two of the fellows up there."

> **Stern:** So, that would be eight including yourself, plus two employees of the railroad. One for the T & P and one of the Katy?
> **Holland:** That's right. At that time. Now, like I said a while ago, by the time they started there was quite a few come up there, but I can't remember who it was or their names, because — [Stern cuts Holland off in mid-sentence here]
> **Stern:** These were people you recognized as employees?
> **Holland:** Some of them, and some of them I did not recognize, but I think he was asking for credentials.
> **Stern:** So, that it is fair to say that at the time of the President's motorcade turned into this area, there was no one on the overpass that you didn't know either as Terminal Co. employees, or railroad employees, or as a policeman?
> **Holland:** Wouldn't be fair to say that, because there was quite a few came up there right in the last moments.

The identities of these unknown persons has remained a mystery since the day of the assassination. The government never pursued this issue and failed to ask the two officers who were assigned to secure the overpass.

Later during Holland's testimony, Mr. Stern asks about the shooting. Holland states,

> **Stern:** Did you hear a third report?
> **Holland:** I heard a third report and I counted four shots and about the same time all this was happening, and in this group of trees—[indicating].
> **Stern:** Now, you are indicating trees on the north side of Elm Street?
> **Holland:** These trees right along here [indicating].
> **Stern:** Let's mark this Exhibit C and draw a circle around the trees you are referring to.

Three different exhibits used during Holland's testimony, each one labeled Holland Exhibit A, B & C (Volume 20, pgs 160-162). Exhibit A is a sketch of the triple underpass originally drawn by Officer Joe Murphy (photo 98); Exhibit B is a black and white photograph taken by Holland showing his son atop the overpass looking east into Dealey Plaza; and Exhibit C is a photo of the book depository taken from the south end of the overpass.

Stern directed Holland to draw a circle on Exhibit C where he saw the puff of smoke. No circle can be found on this document.

> **Holland:** Right in there [indicating]. There was a shot, a report, I don't know whether it was a shot. I can't say that. And a puff of smoke came out about 6 or 8 feet above the ground right from under those trees. And at just about this location from where I was standing you could see that puff of smoke, like someone had thrown a firecracker, or something out, and that is just about the way it sounded. It wasn't as loud as the previous reports or shots.

Dallas police officer Joe Murphy testified to the Warren Commission on April 8, 1964, and made this sketch of Dealey Plaza. The sketch was labeled Murphy Exhibit A and entered into the record. It is not known why the Commission labeled this sketch as 2 different exhibits. This would not be acceptable in any criminal court. Simply because a witness is handed a document, or sketch, if it has previously been entered into the record, the name of the evidence is not changed. If Mr. Stern wanted Holland to indicate points on a map, he should have directed Holland to draw one himself. Why did the government not enlist the services of a professional map maker, or have an aerial photo of Dealey Plaza available for the witnesses?

In the next set of exchanges between these two men, Stern tries to get Holland to recant his statement about hearing four shots.

> **Stern:** Did you tell them [FBI] that you heard distinctly four shots at that time?
> **Holland:** Yes.
> **Stern:** You were certain then?
> **Holland:** I was certain then and I — in that statement I believe that I... (Stern cuts Holland off in mid-sentence).
> **Stern:** Well, the FBI report that I have said that you heard either three or four shots together, and I gather the impression of the agent was that you were uncertain whether it was three or four.
> **Holland:** At the time I made that statement, of course, I was pretty well shook up. But I told the people at the sheriff's office, whoever took my statement, that I believed there was four shots, because they were so close together, and I have also told those two, four, six Federal men that have been out there that I definitely saw the puff of smoke and hear the report from under those trees.
> **Stern:** Did you realize that these were shots then?
> **Holland:** Yes; I think I realized what was happening out there.
> **Stern:** You did?
> **Holland:** When Governor Connally was knocked down in the seat.
> **Stern:** What did you then do?
> **Holland:** Well, immediately after the shots were fired, I run around the end of this overpass, behind the fence to see if I could see anyone up there behind the fence.

Stern: That is the picket fence?

Holland: That is the picket fence.

Stern: On the north side of Elm Street?

Holland: Of course, this was this sea of cars in there and it was just a big—it wasn't an inch in there that wasn't automobiles and I couldn't see up in that corner. I ran on up to the corner of this fence behind the building. By the time I got there there were 12 or 15 policemen and plainclothesmen, and we looked for empty shells around there for quite a while, and I left.

Stern then asks Holland where he thinks the sounds of the shots had come from. Notice now Mr. Stern refers to the shots as "noises."

Stern: What was your impression about the source of these noises, if you had one?

Holland: Well, the impression was that the shots, the first two or three shots came from the upper part of the street from where I was.

Stern: East on Elm?

Holland: Yes, up in here somewhere [indicating] I didn't have the last idea that it was up any higher, but I thought the shots was coming — coming from this crowd in here [indicating]. That is what it sounded like to me from where I was.

It is not known what is meant by "indicating" in Holland's testimony as the record does not specify what this witness was pointing to during his testimony. Normally if a witness refers to something such as a sketch, photograph, or a document, it is mentioned in the court transcripts.

Before Holland concluded his testimony, he is asked by his own attorney if there is anything that he wants to add to the record. Holland then proceeds to tell the government's attorney about what he saw behind the picket fence,

Holland: Well, the only thing that I remember now that I didn't then, I remember about the third car down from this fence, there was station wagon backed up toward the fence, about the third car down, and a spot, I'd say 3 foot by 2 foot, looked to me like somebody had been standing there for a long period. I guess if you could count them about a hundred foottracks in that little spot, and also mud upon the bumper of that station wagon.

Stern: This was a car back, parked behind the picket fence? Well, why don't you put the Number "5" approximately where that car would have been.

The record does not indicate on which document, photograph, or sketch Holland placed the number "5" on to show where he saw this station wagon behind the fence.

Holland: If we could call this the arcade [indicating].

Stern: All right.

Holland: And one, two, three, I think it would have been just about here [indicating].

Stern: All right.

Morrison (Holland's attorney): That is Elm Street. It would be behind the fence, wouldn't it?

Continued on page 178

Photo 97: Marked as Holland Exhibit C, in Volume 20, page 160. No circle is visible on this photograph.

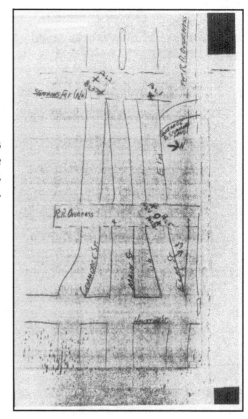

Photo 98: Holland Exhibit A. This exhibit, drawn by Dallas police officer Joe Murphy, was previously entered into the record as Murphy Exhibit A. During Sam Holland's testimony, this sketch was re-marked Holland Exhibit A.

Photo 99: Sam Holland on the triple overpass points toward the picket fence where he saw a puff of smoke on November 22, 1963. A section of the steam pipe is visible in this photo (arrow).

Photo 100: Sam Holland stands on the triple overpass in the same location where he stood on the day of the assassination of President Kennedy.

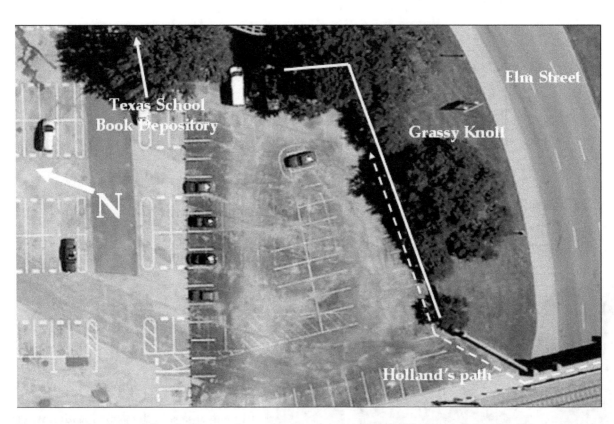

Photo 101: The dashed line indicates the path taken by Sam Holland. The solid white line represents the picket fence.

Photo 102: Sam Holland standing behind the picket fence where he discovered footprints and cigarette butts moments after the assassination.

Photo 103: "Right under these trees...it was just like somebody had thrown a firecracker and left a little puff of smoke there." Sam Holland, November 30, 1966.

Holland: Well, I have got the fence running up here, and this car would be back in there [indicating]. This is the trees out here, which would — and that is approximately the same location as—the car and the trees that I saw the smoke would probably be the same location.

Stern: All right. And this was a station wagon?

Holland: Now, the reason I didn't think so much about that at the time, was because there was so many people out there, and there was law enforcement officers and I thought, well, if there is anything to that they would pick that up, or notice it, but it looks like someone had been standing there for a long time, because it was muddy.

Stern: Tracks you saw in the mud?

Holland: It was muddy, and you could have if you could have counted them, I imagine it would have been a hundred tracks just in that one location. It was just—(Stern cuts Holland off in mid-sentence).

Stern: And then you saw some mud on the bumper?

Holland: Mud on the bumper in two spots.

Stern: As if someone had cleaned his foot, or...

Holland: Well, as if someone had cleaned their foot, or stood up on the bumper to see over the fence.

Near the end of this session with Stern, Holland asked if Stern wanted to know about the actions of two police officers who were riding in the motorcade. Reading the testimony, one gets the impression that this caught Stern off guard. He allowed Holland to tell what he saw,

Holland: Now, do you want to know about the two policemen that were riding in that motorcade and one of them throwed the motorcycle down right in the middle of the street and run up towards that location with his gun in his hand.

Stern: Toward—

Holland: The location that...

Stern: Where you saw the puff of smoke?

Holland: Where I saw the puff of smoke. And another one tried to ride up the hill on his motorcycle and got about halfway up there and he run up the rest of the way on foot.

Stern: Go ahead. This is at the time of the —

Holland: At the time of the...

Stern: That the shots were fired?

Holland: The shots were fired.

Stern: Two motorcycle policemen who were in the motorcade?

Holland: In the motorcade, and one of them threwed his motorcycle down right in the middle of the street and ran up the incline with this pistol in his hand and the other motorcycle policeman jumped over the curb with his motorcycle, and he, tipped over with him up there, and he ran up there the rest of the way with his...(Stern cuts Holland off at this point).

Stern: Did you see anything further involving those two?

Holland: No; I ran around, I was going around the corner of the fence.

Holland is describing the actions of Dallas motorcycle officer Bobby Hargis, who parked his motorcycle against the south curb and ran towards the triple overpass. The other officer was motorcycle officer Clyde Haygood who attempted to ride his motorcycle up the grassy knoll, towards the picket fence.

Assassination researcher and author, Josiah Thompson, conducted a taped interview with Sam Holland on November 30, 1966. In Thompson's book, "Six Seconds in Dallas," (1967), Holland was asked to point to the area on a photograph exactly where he had seen the puff of smoke. Holland stated,

> Right under these trees, right at that exact spot, about 10 or 15 feet from this corner, the corner of the fence here, back this way, right under this clump of trees, right under this tree, particular tree. It's that exact spot, right there...That's where it was...just like somebody had thrown a firecracker and left a little puff of smoke there; it was just laying there. It was a white smoke; it wasn't a black smoke or like a black powder. It was like a puff of a cigarette but it was about nine feet off the ground. It would be just about in the line with, or maybe just a little bit higher than that fence, but by the time it got out underneath the tree, well, it would be about eight or nine feet...[the ground slopes sharply in front of the fence].

In 1967, Thompson interviewed Holland and asked him to describe the scene behind the picket fence when he and several other witnesses arrived there moments after the shooting,

> They [footprints] didn't extend further than from one end of the bumper to the other. That's as far as they would go. It looked like a lion pacing a cage...just to the west of the station wagon there were two sets of footprints...they could've gotten in the trunk compartment of this car and pulled the lid down which would have been very, very easy. ("Six Seconds in Dallas," p. 161)

Holland told that his testimony as printed in the Warren Commission Hearings does not accurately reflect what he stated during his appearance before Counsel Stern. Some weeks after he testified, Holland returned with his attorney and together they corrected the transcript. He told Thompson, "We red marked...red penciled that statement from beginning to end because there were a lot of errors in it. I don't know whether it was made with people attacking it or whether the girl that took the testimony made mistakes. But there were a lot of mistakes in it and we corrected it with a red pencil."

Sam Holland was emphatic in his statements to the Warren Commission about seeing smoke and hearing four gunshots coming from the area of the picket fence. He was adamant about what he saw and heard while standing on the overpass. The FBI and the Warren Commission simply chose to ignore any and all evidence that did not support "the lone gunman scenario."

Key witnesses like Ed Hoffman, Sam Holland, Lee Bowers, Roger Craig, Richard Carr, Marvin Robinson, and Roy Cooper, should have been the starting point for uncovering the truth behind the murder of President Kennedy. They each had pertinent information and gave statements to the authorities. The premise of their account was corroborated by seventy-five additional eyewitnesses. Had the federal government chose to conduct a legitimate and honest criminal investigation, the case could have been solved in a timely manner.

Unfortunately, the local, state, and federal authorities ignored the basic principles of criminal investigation and all of the witnesses who corroborated the statements of Ed Hoffman were ignored. It seemed as if the government had already solved the murder of President Kennedy when the Federal Bureau of Investigation submitted their final report just five days after the assassination. The FBI concluded Lee Harvey Oswald was the lone assassin of President Kennedy and that all the shots had been fired from the book depository.

After the Warren Commission completed its work in September of 1964, it was no surprise they had come to the same conclusion as the FBI. On page 71 of the Warren Report, the final solution was presented to the American people,

> "...The Warren Commission's investigation has disclosed no credible evidence that any shots were fired anywhere other than the Texas School Book Depository Building."

The use of the word "investigation" is problematic. The Commissioners and their appointed counsel were not conducting an investigation; if they had, they would have discovered that over 70% of the witnesses that provided sworn statements, interviewed by the FBI, or testified before the Commission, stated something unusual had occurred in the area on the west side of the Texas School Book Depository.

These witnesses should have been embraced for coming forward with their information; instead, they were ignored, threatened, and even killed because they told the truth. The arrogance of our government in ignoring these witnesses does not uphold the founding principles of a constitutional democracy.

Not only did the Warren Commission fail to adequately investigate this case, the FBI failed as well. Because of their failures, oversights and incompetence, the American public was denied the truth about the murder of President Kennedy.

The Sum of All Fears

"Conspiracy in the assassination of JFK is no longer a theory, but historical fact. JFK was killed by a simulated attack in Dealey Plaza, planned as a test of security but turned into a real attack."

GEORGE MICHAEL EVICA

The purpose of this book is to objectively examine the story of assassination eyewitness, Ed Hoffman. His account of the activity behind the fence is more convincing than the lone gunman in the book depository. Multiple witnesses standing in Dealey Plaza corroborate the same events observed by Ed Hoffman.

Rosie Hoffman, Ed's wife, has communicated to the authors many times, when Ed came home on the afternoon of November 22, she knew something terrible had happened just by the look on his face. He told Rosie he saw a man in a suit fire a rifle in the direction of President Kennedy's motorcade. He described the President's head wound, the blood covering back seat of the limousine, and the man who pointed a machine gun at him.

Author Bill Sloan interviewed Ed's friend, Lucien Pierce. In "JFK: Breaking the Silence," Sloan writes,

> He came straight to where I was working and starting telling me about it. He told me about seeing the man shoot the gun and then seeing the other man take the gun apart. I was shocked and surprised at what he was saying but I didn't have any doubt whether he had actually seen it. He was terrible upset and he kept repeating the story over and over. I knew he wanted to tell the police or the FBI but I could tell he was afraid. (p. 23-24)

Ed's father, Frederick Hoffman, never discussed his son's story outside the immediate family. The Hoffman family *knew* Frederick believed Ed's story from the beginning. Frederick was trying to protect his son from the FBI by deflecting their inquiry.

Robert Hoffman, Ed's uncle, learned of Ed's story that Thanksgiving weekend. Frederick interpreted Ed's story to Robert. As Robert learned more of Ed's story, he decided it would be in the best interest of his nephew, *not* to discuss the events of November 22, 1963. Bill Sloan writes about Robert Hoffman in his book,

> I know that Eddie's a very bright person and always has been, and I can't think of any reason why he would make up something like this. It would be completely out of his character for him to change his story or to add to it at a later date...His father was very, very concerned that Eddie knew anything about the assassination at all. It was time when suspicions were running high and he [Frederick] was worried about Eddie getting involved in any way. (p. 30-31)

It has been an honor and privilege to have known and worked with Ed Hoffman for twenty years. He is a truthful, honest American citizen, and good friend. His character and integrity are above reproach.

Ed Hoffman's basic story of the events he witnessed behind the picket fence on November 22, 1963, has remained consistent for 45 years.

If Ed Hoffman spent *any* time in Dealey Plaza, prior to November 22, 1963, it would be making deliveries for his floral shop. On the day of President Kennedy's murder, Ed did not know there was a picket fence running parallel to Elm Street; he did not know the names of the buildings in the plaza; he never walked in the parking lot on the west side of the Texas School Book Depository; and he did not know about the steam pipe that separated the railroad tracks and the parking lot west of the book depository.

HOW DID ED HOFFMAN KNOW THESE VERIFIABLE FACTS?

- A uniformed police officer *was* stationed on the railroad bridge over Stemmons Freeway;

- At least one uniformed police officer *was* stationed on top of the triple overpass;

- Nearly a dozen men *were* standing on the east side of the triple overpass;

- A Rambler station wagon *did* drive into the parking lot near the book depository.

- This same Rambler station wagon *was* seen at other locations within a 3-block area around Dealey Plaza moments after the shooting;

- A puff of smoke *was* seen at the picket fence;

- A uniformed police officer *did* confront the man in the business suit at gunpoint in the parking lot;

- The President's fatal wound *was* on the back right side of the head;

- A man riding in the President's car *was* standing on the back seat;

- An agent in the follow-up car *was* handling an automatic rifle when it entered the on-ramp of Stemmons Freeway.

The answer is simple. On November 22, 1963, between 12 noon. and 12:40 pm., Ed Hoffman *was* standing on the west side of Stemmons Freeway, and *did* see a man fire a rifle in the direction of President Kennedy's motorcade.

The Dallas police department and the FBI, ignored witnesses who said they heard gunshots coming from the area of the picket fence on the grassy knoll. The government decided the statements of seventy-eight witness who believed shots had been fired from this area were not worthy of follow-up. Thirty-one of the seventy-eight witnesses listed in this book appeared before the Warren Commission.

The official FBI reports of Ed Hoffman's eyewitness account are inconsistent and do not accurately reflect the information he provided. *Some* issues of inaccuracy can be explained by the fact that no sign language interpreter was present during the interviews.

Ed's first interview with FBI Special Agent Will Griffin, led to further interviews with Ed's father and brother. FBI Director J. Edgar Hoover, ordered his agents to establish if Ed Hoffman was a "credible witness." Hundreds of witnesses were interviewed by the FBI during this investigation, and Ed Hoffman's credibility may be the only one questioned in this manner.

Ed Hoffman, and the hundreds of spectators, witnessed a coup d'état in Dealey Plaza, on November 22, 1963. This was a sudden and violent overthrow of the American government. Those involved in this conspiracy hoped their part would go unpunished. Ed Hoffman witnessed a large part of this criminal act and told people about it that same day.

The best explanation of President Kennedy's assassination was summarized in the words of New Orleans District Attorney, Jim Garrison (1921-1992), who wrote,

> A coup d'etat has been described as a 'sudden action by which an individual or group, usually employing limited violence, captures positions of governmental authority without conforming to the formal requirement for changing officeholders, as prescribed by the laws or constitution.
>
> A successful coup requires a number of elements; extensive planning and preparation by the sponsors (those responsible for the coup); the collaboration of the Praetorian Guard (officials whose job is to protect the government, including the President); a diversionary cover-up afterwards; (the Warren Commission); the ratification of the assassination by the new government inheriting power; and the dissemination of disinformation by major elements of the news media. If this concurrence of events has a familiar sound, it is because this is exactly what happened when John Kennedy was murdered. ("On the Trail of the Assassins," 1988, p. 324-325)

Ed Hoffman's account of the murder of President Kennedy establishes him as the most important eyewitness to this crime. His account is truthful, and does not conform to the federal government's final script. Instead of embracing this important witness, Ed Hoffman was misunderstood by the FBI, misinterpreted by researchers, and crucified by the media.

His complete story and eyewitness account should be evaluated for what it is — *THE TRUTH!*

Thank you, Ed Hoffman!

APPENDIX A:
Eyewitness Maps

"After the shots were fired, I turned towards the knoll...puffs of smoke were still hanging in the air in small patches, but no one was visible."

CHERYL MCKINNON

Dealey Plaza, Dallas, Texas
Base Map

Section Ⓐ

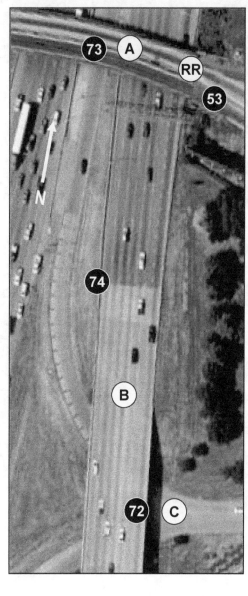

Ⓐ	Texas & Pacific RR Bridge
Ⓑ	Stemmons Freeway I-35N East
Ⓒ	Elm St. Entrance Ramp
53	DPD Officer Earle Brown
72	DPD Officer Joe Murphy
73	DPD Officer Lomax
74	Ed Hoffman

Ⓡ

Ⓡ

Ⓡ

Section Ⓑ

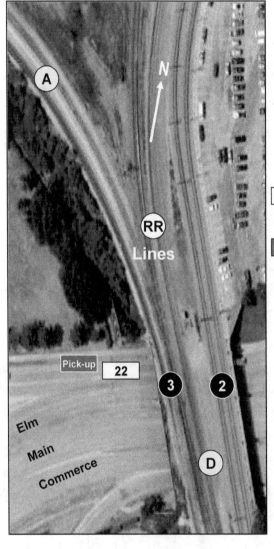

Ⓐ Texas & Pacific
RR Bridge

Ⓓ Triple Underpass

2 DPD Officer Foster

3 DPD Officer White

22 Julia Ann Mercer
11am 11/22/63

Pick-up Green Pick-up truck
blocking traffic 11am.

Ⓡ

Ⓡ

Ⓡ

Section Ⓒ

Ⓓ Triple Underpass

② J.W. Foster

③ J.C. White

④ Sam Holland

⑤ Richard Dodd

⑥ Walther Windborn

⑦ Curtis Bishop

⑧ Ewell Cowsert

⑨ Royce Skelton

⑩ Clemon Johnson

⑪ Austin Miller

⑫ Frank Reilly

⑬ James Simmons

⑭ Nolan Potter

⑮ Thomas Murphy

㊷ James Tague

Section Ⓓ

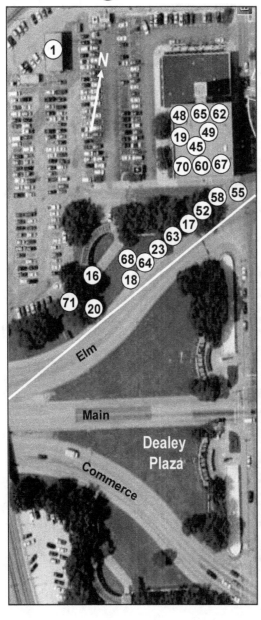

- **1** Lee Bowers
- **16** Abraham Zapruder
- **17** A.J. Milican
- **18** William Newman
- **19** Ochus Campbell
- **20** Emmett Hudson
- **23** Jean Newman
- **45** Joe Molina
- **48** Victoria Adams
- **49** Billy Lovelady
- **48** Victoria Adams
- **52** Clyde Haygood
- **55** Ron Fischer
- **58** Roy Truly
- **60** Otis Williams
- **62** Steve Williams
- **63** Mary Woodward
- **64** Maggie Brown
- **65** Elsie Dorman
- **67** Roy Lewis
- **68** Cheryl McKinnon
- **70** William Shelly
- **71** Gordon Arnold

Section (E)

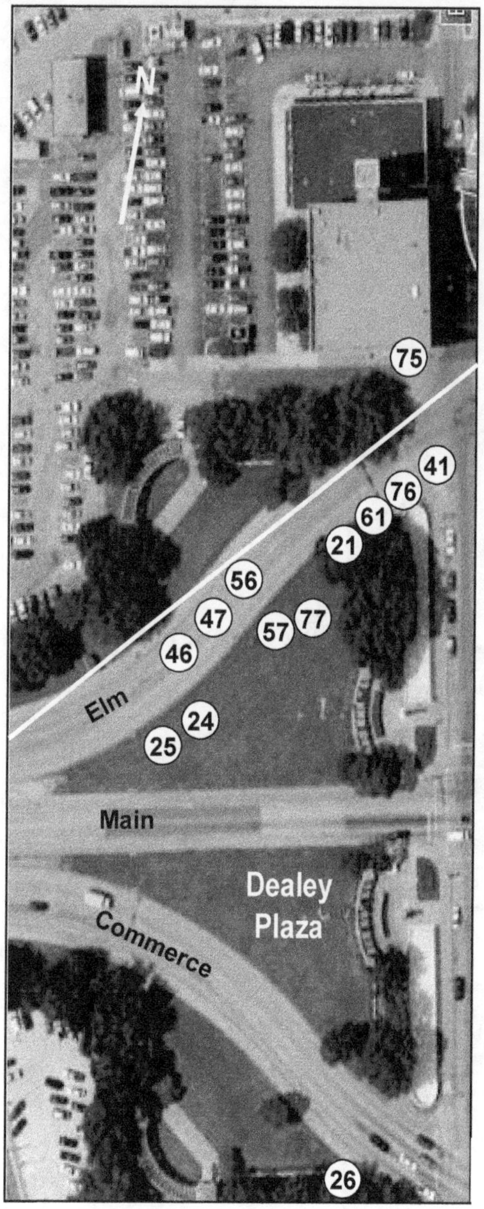

(21) Delores Koumae
(24) Malcolm Summers
(25) Jack Franzen
(26) J.C. Price
(41) Ralph Yarborough
(46) Roy Kellerman
(47) Clint Hill
(56) Bobby Hargis
(57) Jean Hill
(61) Phil Willis
(75) Virgie Rackley
(76) Mrs. James Reece
(77) Beverly Oliver (Massagee)

Section Ⓕ

Ⓔlm Street
54 51
43
Houston Street
44
69
78
50
59
66
Main Street
27 40

② W.W. Mabra

④ Jack Faulkner

④ D.V. Harkness

④ Arnold Rowland

⑤ Marion Baker

⑤ Edgar Smith

⑤ Joe Marshall Smith

⑤ Robert West

⑥ Wayne & Edna Hartman

⑥ Sam Paternostro

⑦ Hollis B. McLain

APPENDIX B
Documents

"I initially heard three shots during the assassination. At the time of the shooting, I felt that all three shots had come from the fence area on top of the knoll."

ORVILLE NIX

Document 1:

This is a cover letter from Special Agent in Charge of the Dallas office to the Director regarding the first interview of Ed Hoffman that occurred on June 28, 1967. The agent conducting the interview was Will Hayden Griffin.

Document 2:

The first paragraph of this report deals with one of Ed's supervisors at Texas Instruments who had set up the interview. The last sentence of this paragraph states,

> It was pointed out to Mr. Dowdy that Hoffman should put in writing in detail everything he saw the day of the assassination.

There are four possible scenarios for this miscommunication,

- The agent did not tell Dowdy to have Ed bring a written statement to the interview, and the agent falsified his report;

- The agent did tell Dowdy, but Dowdy failed to mention it to Ed;

- Dowdy did tell Ed about the agent's desire for a written statement and Ed brought it with him to the interview; or,

- The written statement did exist but it was kept out of Ed's official FBI file.

In the second paragraph, Agent Griffin writes,

> ...[Ed] parked his automobile near the railroad tracks on Stemmons Freeway in Dallas, north of the intersection of Stemmons Freeway and Elm Street.

Ed has always maintained he parked his car several car lengths south of the railroad bridge that crosses over Stemmons Freeway. When he exited his car, he looked up and saw a uniformed police officer on the bridge.

In the third paragraph, Agent Griffin writes,

> Hoffman said he was standing a few feet south of the railroad on Stemmons Freeway when the motorcade passed...Hoffman walked south along the west shoulder of Stemmons Freeway and stood above the Elm Street entrance ramp. He was approximately 100 yards south of the railroad bridge. One hundred yards is quite different than a "few feet." Either Griffin deliberately misrepresented what Hoffman told him, or misunderstood what Hoffman was attempting to convey to him during the interview. If Ed stood "a few feet south" of the railroad, he would not have been in a position to see the activity behind the fence. It is not known why Griffin wrote "a few feet" instead of the true distance.

The report then states,

> Hoffman said he observed two white males, clutching something dark to their chests with both hands, running from the rear of the Texas School Book Depository building.

Hoffman denies that he ever mentioned seeing anyone running out of the back of the book depository to anyone, including any FBI agent. It is possible that the agent misunderstood what Ed was describing, or deliberately misrepresented the information in his report.

Document 3:

This is page 2 of the FBI report filed by Agent Griffin. It states that two hours after the interview, Ed had returned from where he had stood on Stemmons freeway on November 22. The report states that Ed,

> ...decided that he could not have seen the men running because of a fence west of the Texas School Depository building.

Not until Ed was able to obtain his FBI file through the Freedom of Information Act, he was not aware this information was attributed to him. Hoffman does admit that he returned to the FBI office later that day, but it was only to clarify his earlier statement. Ed denies he told Agent Griffin that the fence blocked his view of the activity in the parking lot.

Document 4:

This document, dated July 3, 1967, is from Hoover to Gordon Shanklin, Special Agent in Charge of the Dallas field office. FBI Director Hoover wanted Shanklin's agents to "fully resolve" four issues concerning Ed's interview with Agent Griffin.

> a) The "alleged" sighting of men running "from the rear of the Texas School Book Depository building immediately after the assassination"; b) whether or not a fence was where Hoffman said there was; c) interview Hoffman's father to determine if Ed's story "has credence"; and, d) determine if there were any other witnesses who saw anyone running from the rear of the book depository.

Document 5:

This FBI report is the response to the Director's order to clear up the four issues listed on document #4. The agents apparently did not go to the site to determine for themselves if a fence was there, but instead interviewed Roy Truly, the manager of the book depository. It is not known where this interview took place. It is not known why the agents interviewed the manager of the book depository regarding whether or not a fence was in the area. It is not known if these agents walked the parking lot in order to locate specific landmarks. According to the FBI report, Roy Truly advised the agents that,

…there is a fence approximately 6 feet tall running from the parking lot west of the Texas School Book Depository for about 150 feet to the north of the Texas School Book Depository.

Walking directly west from the west side of the book depository to a point even with the west end of the fence is 175 feet. From this location, the picket fence is 100 feet to the south. The picket fence runs *east and west*, not north. (See photo 107 below.)

Why were agents directed to determine if Ed was a credible witness? Did they interview the family members of any other witness? What information did Ed tell Agent Griffin that made Hoover direct his agents to ascertain if Ed was telling the truth? The FBI report dated June 28, 1967 states that Ed,

> …observed two white males running from the rear of the Texas School Book Depository building.

This statement is problematic on several points. One, Hoffman denies he ever said he saw anyone running from the rear of the building after the shooting. The report continues,

> Virgil Hoffman told them (Ed's father and brother) he saw numerous men running after the President was shot.

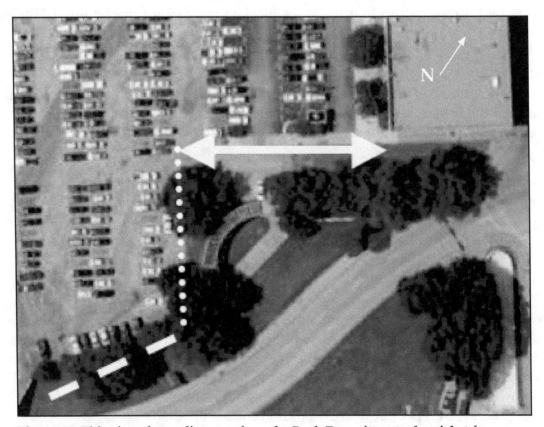

Photo 107: This view shows distances from the Book Depository to the picket fence.

Many of the witnesses present in Dealey Plaza saw people running after the shooting. This statement of "seeing people running after the shots" was allegedly made by Frederick and Fred Hoffman, not Ed.

The FBI report then states, "The father of Virgil Hoffman stated that he did not believe that his son had seen anything of value and doubted he had observed any men running from the Texas School Book Depository." In a routine criminal investigation, only provable facts are included in a report.

An expert can provide his opinion, but it must be based on factual data. If the subject of the interview provides an opinion based on anything other than facts, the opinion is considered heresay. This type of evidence would not be admitted into a court of law.

Document 6:

This is the cover letter dated April 5, 1977, from the Dallas Special Agent in Charge to the FBI Director. It is in response to a second interview of Ed Hoffman by the FBI. It states Ed Hoffman was interviewed by Agent Griffin on June 28, 1967. The agent's name conducting this second interview has been blacked out of the report. We know from other FBI reports this agent was Udo H. Specht. Agent Specht gave Hoffman his business card after the interview. It is not known why Specht's name has been deleted from the report.

Document 7:

The first paragraph of this two page report is information obtained from another supervisor at Texas Instruments who contacted the FBI on March 21, 1977, and related that Ed Hoffman had information about the assassination.

The remainder of the document is a summary of the 1967 interview. No new information was noted on this FBI report.

Document 8:

The first two paragraphs of this page are a continuation of the summary of Hoffman's 1967 interview. The last paragraph on this page is new information which was not included in the 1967 report.

> Hoffman said the only description he could furnish of the men was that one of them wore a white shirt.

Document 9:

This is page 3 of Agent Specht's 1977 field report. The first two paragraphs are a summary of the 1967 interview. However, in the last paragraph of this report, Specht writes,

> On March 21, 1977, Virgil E. Hoffman...voluntarily appeared at the Dallas FBI Office and Special Agent (name blacked out) attempted to communicate with him. Special Agent (name blacked out) had a great deal of difficulty communicating with Mr. Hoffman since he is a deaf mute, does not read lips, and appears to be semi-illiterate in the reading and writing of the English language.

Document 10:

> This is page 4 of Agent Specht's field report. New information appears in this report which was not mentioned in Griffin's original 1967 report.

> ...he saw two men, one with a rifle and one with a handgun, behind a wooden fence at the moment he saw the presidential motorcade speed north on Stemmons Freeway. Hoffman made hand motions indicating that one of the men disassembled the rifle and placed it in a suitcase or similar container. Hoffman indicated that he saw smoke prior to that. The two men ran north on the railroad tracks and he lost sight of them.

Hoffman has maintained when he saw the man in the business suit toss the rifle to yardman, he saw what may have been some type of shoulder holster under his suit jacket. The man in the business suit carried the rifle with both hands and tossed the weapon to yard man using an underhanded motion. Hoffman communicated he saw the man in the business suit's shoulder holster when he tossed the rifle.

Ed has maintained that the only person he saw walking briskly north along the railroad tracks was yard man after he placed the rifle into the tool box/bag. The man in the business suit walked *casually* back to the fence after tossing the rifle. The man in the business suit was confronted at gunpoint by uniformed officer Joe Marshall Smith moments after the shooting.

Document 11:

> This three-page report, dated March 25, 1977, was filed by Agent Udo Specht, even though his name is blacked out of the report. This report deals with Richard Freeman, another supervisor at Texas Instruments. This report is Freeman's version of Ed's story as told to Agent Specht.

> Freeman attempted to tell Agent Specht everything that Hoffman told him as accurately as possible. It is not known if Freeman actually visited Dealey Plaza before meeting with Agent Specht because some references to landmarks are incorrect. This could be blamed on Freeman's unfamiliarity with the area, or Agent Specht misunderstood what Freeman was telling him. Specht writes,

> Hoffman saw two men, one with a rifle and one with a handgun, behind a wooden fence, approximately six feet in height. This fence is located on the same side of Elm Street as the Texas School Book Depository building but closer to Stemmons Freeway.

According to Hoffman, only *one* man was behind the wooden fence when the shooting occurred. In addition, the choice of word usage in the second sentence makes it difficult to visualize where the fence is located in reference to the book depository. The use of the word "closer" is confusing. Is Freeman suggesting that the fence is closer to Stemmons Freeway than to Elm Street? The east end of the fence is 250 yards from Stemmons Freeway.

This FBI report does mention Freeman was told by Hoffman he saw smoke in the area. The problem with this statement is *where* Freeman told the FBI that Ed communicated he saw the smoke.

...he saw a puff of smoke in the vicinity of where the two men were standing... the puff of smoke in the vicinity of the two men.

The man in the business suit and yard man were *not* together when the shot was fired. Ed only saw smoke near where the man in the business suit was standing at the fence. This is the *only* area where Hoffman recalls seeing smoke that day. The FBI report continues,

...the man with the rifle looked like he was breaking the rifle down by removing the barrel from the stock and placing it in some dark type of suitcase that the other man was holding.

Only yard man took the rifle apart and placed it in a tool box or soft bag. Hoffman has never mentioned the color of the tool box/bag. Did Freeman repeat what Ed told him, or did Freeman just assume the box/bag was dark? After tossing the rifle to yard man, the man in the business suit man walked casually back towards the fence.

...The two men then ran north on the railroad tracks by actually running on the tracks.

Only yard man left the area by walking north along or on the railroad tracks. This man was "walking briskly" when Hoffman saw him and if he did run, it could have been after he was out of Ed's line of sight.

The last two sentences on FBI report state,

Hoffman was standing approximately 75 yards from this fence. This fence was at approximately the same height or level as the ground floor of the Texas School Book Depository.

Several possibilities can be deduced from the information in these two sentences,

- Freeman visited Dealey Plaza before he called Specht and estimated the distance and elevation on his own;

- Freeman *did not* visit Dealey Plaza and made an educated guess of the distance and elevation based on what Hoffman communicated to him, and then relayed the information to Specht;

- Specht went to Dealey Plaza and estimated the distance and elevation for himself; or,

- Hoffman estimated the distance and elevation and communicated that information to Freeman before or while Freeman was on the phone to Specht.

Regardless, the distance from Hoffman's location to the closest point of the picket fence was *215 yards*, not *75 yards*. However, the fence *is* on the same level as the ground floor of the book depository.

Document 12:

This is page two of Agent Specht's 1977 report. The first paragraph contains information not reported in Agent Griffin's original 1967 FBI report. Specht writes,

> Both men were white males, both dressed in some type of white suits, and both wore ties.

This is the first time a clothing description is mentioned in any FBI report. This is either a misinterpretation between Hoffman and Freeman, a misunderstanding between Freeman and Specht, or a deliberate misrepresentation in Specht's report.

Specht's report continues,

> There were no other people in his area of observation, not in the area where the two men were standing behind the fence.

Ed has maintained he saw a uniformed police officer standing at the north corner of the fence before the shooting. This officer was *not* wearing a hat and was *not* the same officer who pointed his pistol at the man in the business suit moments after the shooting.

The second paragraph of this FBI report states Specht was contacted by Freeman via telephone on March 28, to make an appointment for Hoffman. The report states Ed and Specht met later that same day and went out to Stemmons freeway.

The FBI report does not indicate if Freeman went with Ed to act as interpreter.

The last paragraph of this FBI report is a summary of what Ed communicated to Specht. Surprisingly, this paragraph, for the most part, accurately describes what Ed saw on November 22, 1963. The incorrect information is about the two men running north on the railroad tracks. If now sign language interpreter was present, how was Specht able to record this much information so precisely? Did Specht understand American Sign Language?

Document 13:

This is page 3 of Specht's FBI report. In the next to last paragraph, Specht writes he took color photographs from Stemmons Freeway, north of the grassy knoll, and the area adjacent to it. The last sentence in this paragraph, Specht writes,

> The distance from where Mr. Hoffman was viewing the motorcade on Stemmons Freeway to the area behind the wooden fence is estimated at approximately (the typed number "280" is crossed out and replaced with the hand-written figure "105"), yards, with the elevation being approximately the same height as the first floor of the Texas School Book Depository building.

Recall the true distance between Hoffman's location on Stemmons Freeway and the closest point of the fence is 215 yards. Agent Specht describes the type of camera he used, the brand and type of film, and the settings of the camera. However, none of these photographs has ever been seen and no photographs are included in Hoffman's FBI file.

Document 14:

This is a copy of FBI Special Agent Udo H. Specht's business card he gave to Ed at the conclusion of their meeting in 1977.

Document 15:

This is the letter Ed sent to Senator Ted Kennedy on October 3, 1975.

Document 16:

This is the letter Hoffman received from Senator Ted Kennedy in response to his letter of October 3rd. The letter is dated November 19th.

Document 17:

This is a copy of the receipt for certified mail on the letter Hoffman sent to the House Senate Select Committee on Assassinations (Ed no longer has a copy of this letter).

The letter was postmarked January 8, 1979. The letter was accepted on January 19, 1979. Hoffman wrote the letter advising the committee he would be available as a witness to the events of November 22, 1963. Unfortunately, the letter arrived after the committee had concluded their investigation.

Document 18:

This letter, dated October 8, 1992, was sent on Ed's behalf to the Dallas FBI office requesting a copy of his complete FBI file. Although the letter is signed by Hoffman, it was not written by him . The letter was received by a person named "Annie D. Hendrix" on October 13, 1992.

Document 19:

This letter is from the Dallas FBI field office and dated October 21, 1992. It is in response to Hoffman's request for his complete FBI file. According to the letter, the Dallas office had no record of any such file under his name (It is very likely that files relating to the assassination were forwarded to FBI headquarters in Washington, DC)

Document 20:

This certified letter, dated October 27, 1992, was addressed to the Washington, DC office of the FBI. The letter was postmarked in Grand Prairie on October 29, 1992. The letter requests a copy of Ed's FBI file be forwarded to him, including any photographs related to his FBI interview in 1977. Although Hoffman signed this letter, it was not written by him.

Document 21:

This letter, dated February 18, 1994 from Jim Marrs to Hoffman's minister, Ron Friedrich. In the letter, Marr's discusses his frustration in obtaining files from the FBI, and their habit of misquoting witnesses. Marrs tells Friedrich,

> The best thing from this point on is to focus on Mr. Hoffman's story and see that it reaches the broadest possible audience.

Document 1

F B I

Date: 6/28/67

Transmit the following in _____
                              (Type in plaintext or code)

AIRTEL _____
                              (Priority)

TO   DIRECTOR, FBI (62-109060)

FROM   SAC, DALLAS (89-43)(P)

RE: ASSASSINATION OF PRESIDENT
          JOHN FITZGERALD KENNEDY
          DALLAS, TEXAS, 11/22/63
          MISCELLANEOUS -
          INFORMATION CONCERNING
          OFFICE OF ORIGIN
          OO: DALLAS

          enclosed are 10 copies of a letterhead memorandum
reflecting results of an interview with VIRGIL E. HOFFMAN,
424 Grand Prairie Road, Grand Prairie, Texas, employed by
Texas Instruments, Dallas, Texas. The interview was conducted by SA WILL HAYDEN GRIFFIN on 6/28/67.

          62-109060-5465

③ - Bureau (Enc. 10) ENCLOSURE
2 - Dallas
WHG/bfm
(5)

          Approved: _____ Sent _____ M _____ Per _____
                    Special Agent in Charge

Document 2

UNITED STATES DEPARTMENT OF JUSTICE

FEDERAL BUREAU OF INVESTIGATION

In Reply, Please Refer to
File No.

Dallas, Texas
June 28, 1967

ASSASSINATION OF PRESIDENT
JOHN FITZGERALD KENNEDY
DALLAS, TEXAS, November 22, 1963

On June 26, 1967, Mr. Jim Dowdy, 725 McLemore,
Garland, Texas, supervisor at Texas Instruments, Dallas,
Texas, advised a deaf mute, Virgil E. Hoffman, who is
employed at Texas Instruments, had indicated he wanted to
furnish information to Agents of the Federal Bureau of
Investigation regarding the assassination of President
John Fitzgerald Kennedy. It was pointed out to Mr. Dowdy
that Hoffman should put in writing in detail everything he
saw the day of the assassination.

On June 28, 1967, Virgil E. Hoffman appeared at
the Dallas Office of the FBI and advised he resided at 424
Grand Prairie Road, Grand Prairie, Texas, and was employed
at Texas Instruments, Dallas. He said he parked his automobile near the railroad tracks on Stemmons Freeway in
Dallas, north of the intersection of Stemmons Freeway and
Elm Street, about 12:00 noon on November 22, 1963.

Hoffman said he was standing a few feet south of
the railroad on Stemmons Freeway when the motorcade passed
him taking President Kennedy to Parkland Hospital. Hoffman
said he observed two white males, clutching something dark
to their chests with both hands, running from the rear of
the Texas School Book Depository building. The men were
running north on the railroad, then turned east, and Hoffman
lost sight of both of the men.

This document contains neither recommendations nor
conclusions of the FBI. It is the property of the
FBI and is loaned to your agency; it and its contents
are not to be distributed outside your agency.

COPIES DESTROYED

4 8 JAN 15 1973   62-109060-5465

ENCLOSURE

180-10024-10407   FBI INVEST. GATIVE FILE ON ASSASSINATION OF J. KENNEDY
62-109060-5465

Document 3

ASSASSINATION OF PRESIDENT
JOHN FITZGERALD KENNEDY

Approximately two hours after the above interview
with Hoffman, he returned to the Dallas Office of the FBI
and advised he had just returned from the spot on Stemmons
Freeway where he had parked his automobile and had decided
he could not have seen the men running because of a fence
west of the Texas School Book Depository building. He said
it was possible that he saw these two men on the fence or
something else

Hoffman said the only description he could furnish
of the men was that one of them wore a white shirt. He
stated he had discussed this matter with his father at the
time of the assassination, and his father suggested that he
not talk to anyone about this, but after thinking about
what he saw, Hoffman stated he decided to tell the FBI.

160-10021 - 10405   FBI INVESTIGATIVE FILE ON ASSASSINATION OF J KENNEDY
62-109....

Document 4

7/3/67

3 — Mr. Gordon

AIRTEL

To: SAC, Dallas   (09-43)
From: Director FBI   (62-109060) — *5465*

ASSASSINATION OF PRESIDENT
JOHN FITZGERALD KENNEDY
DALLAS, TEXAS, 11/22/63
MISCELLANEOUS
INFORMATION CONCERNING
OO: DL

ReDLairtel and LHM 6/28/67.

Dallas is to fully resolve the matter of Virgil E.
Hoffman allegedly seeing two white males running from the rear
of the Texas School Book Depository building immediately
following the assassination of President Kennedy as set out
in Dallas LHM 6/28/67.

Advise Bureau whether (1) Virgil E. Hoffman was
interviewed during the assassination investigation and if
is the information contained in LHM dated 6/28/67, contradictory to information furnished in the previous interview.
(2) Was there a fence located where Virgil E. Hoffman said
there was at the time of the assassination. (3) Virgil E.
Hoffman's father should be interviewed to determine how much
credence can be placed in Virgil E. Hoffman's story. (4) Were
there any other witnesses located and interviewed during the
assassination investigation who supposedly saw someone running
from the rear of the Texas School Book Depository building.
Upon completion of the above investigation, submit results to
Bureau in form suitable for dissemination.

JCC:jc
(4)

SEE NOTE PAGE TWO

Document 5

UNITED STATES DEPARTMENT OF JUSTICE

FEDERAL BUREAU OF INVESTIGATION

In Reply, Please Refer to
File No.

Dallas, Texas
July 6, 1967

ASSASSINATION OF PRESIDENT
JOHN FITZGERALD KENNEDY,
DALLAS, TEXAS,
NOVEMBER 22, 1963

Virgil E. Hoffman was not interviewed prior to
June 28, 1967.

On July 6, 1967, Roy S. Truly, Manager, Texas
School Book Depository, advised there is a fence approximately 6 feet tall running from the parking lot west of
the Texas School Book Depository for about 150 feet to
the north of the Texas School Book Depository. This fence
was constructed approximately two years prior to the assassination and has not been moved to date.

On July 5, 1967, Mr. E. Hoffman, father of Virgil
E. Hoffman, and Fred Hoffman, brother of Virgil Hoffman,
were interviewed at 428 West Main Street, Grand Prairie,
Texas. Both advised that Virgil Hoffman has been a deaf
mute his entire life and has in the past distorted facts
of events observed by him. Both the father and brother
stated that Virgil Hoffman loved President Kennedy and
had mentioned to them just after the assassination that
he (Virgil Hoffman) was standing on the freeway near the
Texas School Book Depository at the time of the assassination. Virgil Hoffman told them he saw numerous men running
after the President was shot. The father of Virgil Hoffman
stated that he did not believe that his son had seen anything
of value and doubted he had observed any men running from
the Texas School Book Depository and for this reason had
not mentioned it to the FBI.

COPIES DESTROYED

54 JAN 15 1973

contents are not to be distributed outside your
agency.

ENCLOSURE

180-10021-10466 FBI IN TEST FILE ON ASSASSINATION OF
62-139060-5624 JOHN KENNEDY

Document 6

```
                                    F B I

                                  Date:    4/5/77

Transmit the following in _____
                            (Type in plaintext or code)

in ___ AIRTEL _____
                          (Precedence)
```

TO: DIRECTOR, FBI (62-109061)

FROM: SAC, DALLAS (89-43) (P)

SUBJECT: ASSASSINATION OF PRESIDENT
           JOHN FITZGERALD KENNEDY,
           NOVEMBER 22, 1963
           DALLAS, TEXAS
           MISCELLANEOUS - INFORMATION CONCERNING
           OO: DALLAS

           Enclosed herewith for the Bureau is the
original and four copies of an LHM dated and captioned
as above.

           SA WILL HAYDEN GRIFFIN, Dallas, Texas, interviewed
Mr. VIRGIL E. HOFFMAN on 6/28/67, as set forth in Dallas
LHM dated 6/28/67. SA GRIFFIN advised SA ███████████
that he no longer has any personal recollection concerning
his interview with Mr. HOFFMAN.

           On Pages 71-76 of the "Report of the President's
Commission on the Assassination of President John F.
Kennedy", the witnesses at the Triple Underpass are
discussed, but the Warren Commission's investigation
has disclosed no credible evidence that any shots were
fired from anywhere other than the Texas School Book
Depository building.

           In view of the above, the Dallas Office is conducting
no additional investigation, UACB.

2-Bureau (Enc. 5)
2-Dallas
UHS:tjd
(4)

Approved: _____   Sent _____ M   Per _____
          Special Agent in Charge

Document 7

UNITED STATES DEPARTMENT OF JUSTICE

FEDERAL BUREAU OF INVESTIGATION

In Reply, Please Refer to
File No.

Dallas, Texas
April 5, 1977

ASSASSINATION OF PRESIDENT
JOHN FITZGERALD KENNEDY,
NOVEMBER 22, 1963,
DALLAS, TEXAS

On March 21, 1977, Tom Cordner, Semi-Conductor Building, Texas Instruments, Richardson, Texas, telephone 238-3885, advised that he works with a deaf mute by the name of Virgil E. Hoffman, who has a great deal of difficulty communicating but who has given him indications that he knows something concerning the President Kennedy Assassination.

A review of Dallas FBI files reflected the following information concerning Virgil E. Hoffman, as set forth in Dallas FBI memorandum dated June 28, 1967, captioned as above:

"On June 26, 1967, Mr. Jim Dowdy, 725 McLemore, Garland, Texas, supervisor at Texas Instruments, Dallas, Texas, advised a deaf mute, Virgil E. Hoffman, who is employed at Texas Instruments, had indicated he wanted to furnish information to Agents of the Federal Bureau of Investigation regarding the assassination of President John Fitzgerald Kennedy. It was pointed out to Mr. Dowdy that Hoffman should put in writing in detail everything he saw the day of the assassination.

"On June 28, 1967, Virgil E. Hoffman appeared at the Dallas Office of the FBI and advised he resided at 424 Grand Prairie Road, Grand Prairie, Texas, and was employed at Texas Instruments, Dallas. He said he parked his automobile near the railroad tracks on Stemmons Freeway in

This document contains neither recommendations nor conclusions of the FBI. It is the property of the FBI and is loaned to your agency; it and its contents are not to be distributed outside your agency.

ENCLOSURE

Document 8

RE: ASSASSINATION OF PRESIDENT
      JOHN FITZGERALD KENNEDY

Dallas, north of the intersection of Stemmons Freeway
and Elm Street, about 12:00 noon on November 22, 1963.

"Hoffman said he was standing a few feet south of
the railroad on Stemmons Freeway when the motorcade passed
him taking President Kennedy to Parkland Hospital. Hoffman
said he observed two white males, clutching something dark
to their chests with both hands, running from the rear of
the Texas School Book Depository building. The men were
running north on the railroad, then turned east, and Hoffman
lost sight of both of the men.

"Approximately two hours after the above interview
with Hoffman, he returned to the Dallas Office of the FBI
and advised he had just returned from the spot on Stemmons
Freeway where he had parked his automobile and had decided
he could not have seen the men running because of a fence
west of the Texas School Book Depository building. He
said it was possible that he saw these two men on the fence
or something else.

- "Hoffman said the only description he could furnish
of the men was that one of them wore a white shirt. He
stated he had discussed this matter with his father at the
time of the assassination, and his father suggested that he
not talk to anyone about this, but after thinking about
what he saw, Hoffman stated he decided to tell the FBI."

The following information was set forth in
Dallas FBI memorandum dated July 6, 1967:

"Virgil E. Hoffman was not interviewed prior to
June 28, 1967.

2

Document 9

RE: ASSASSINATION OF PRESIDENT
JOHN FITZGERALD KENNEDY

"On July 6, 1967, Roy S. Truly, Manager, Texas School Book Depository, advised there is a fence approximately 6 feet tall running from the parking lot west of the Texas School Book Depository for about 150 feet to the north of the Texas School Book Depository. This fence was constructed approximately two years prior to the assassination and has not been moved to date.

"On July 5, 1967, Mr. E. Hoffman, father of Virgil E. Hoffman, and Fred Hoffman, brother of Virgil Hoffman, were interviewed at 428 West Main Street, Grand Prairie, Texas. Both advised that Virgil Hoffman has been a deaf mute his entire life and has in the past distorted facts of events observed by him. Both the father and brother stated that Virgil Hoffman loved President Kennedy and had mentioned to them just after the assassination that he (Virgil Hoffman) was standing on the freeway near the Texas School Book Depository at the time of the assassination. Virgil Hoffman told them he saw numerous men running after the President was shot. The father of Virgil Hoffman stated that he did not believe that his son had seen anything of value and doubted he had observed any men running from the Texas School Book Depository and for this reason had not mentioned it to the FBI."

On March 21, 1977, Virgil E. Hoffman, 424 Grand Prairie Road, Grand Prairie, Texas, voluntarily appeared at the Dallas FBI Office and Special Agent [   ] attempted to communicate with him. Special Agent [   ] had a great deal of difficulty communicating with Mr. Hoffman since he is a deaf mute, does not read lips, and appears to be semi-illiterate in the reading and writing of the English language.

3

180-10024-10233   FBI CASE FILE   62-109060-7722

Document 10

RE: ASSASSINATION OF PRESIDENT
     JOHN FITZGERALD KENNEDY

     Mr. Hoffman attempted to communicate the same basic information that he previously furnished to the Dallas FBI, as set forth in Dallas FBI memorandum dated June 28, 1967. In addition to that information, Hoffman attempted to communicate that he saw two men, one with a rifle and one with a handgun, behind a wooden fence at the moment he saw the presidential motorcade speed north on Stemmons Freeway. Hoffman made hand motions indicating that one of the men disassembled the rifle and placed it in a suitcase or similar container. Hoffman indicated that he saw smoke prior to that. The two men ran north on the railroad tracks and he lost sight of them.

    Hoffman also made available a copy of the following letters:

4

Document 11

RE: ASSASSINATION OF PRESIDENT
    JOHN FITZGERALD KENNEDY

On March 25, 1977, Richard H. Freeman, Texas
Instruments, Semi-Conductor Building, Richardson, Texas,
telephone number 238-4965, home address 2573 Shell,
Frisco, Texas, telephone 377-9456, telephonically advised
Special Agent ████████████ that he knew sign language
and has communicated with Virgil E. Hoffman, a deaf mute
who is employed at his building at Texas Instruments.
Mr. Hoffman communicated with him by the use of sign language
and Hoffman was concerned that the FBI perhaps did not
fully understand what he was trying to communicate. Hoffman
communicated the following information to Mr. Freeman:

Hoffman was watching the motorcade of President
John F. Kennedy on November 22, 1963, at Dallas, Texas.
Hoffman was standing on Stemmons Freeway watching the
presidential motorcade, looking in an easterly direction
when the motorcade sped away and headed north on Stemmons
Freeway. Hoffman communicated that this must have been
right after President Kennedy was shot. Hoffman saw two
men, one with a rifle and one with a handgun, behind a wooden
fence, approximately six feet in height, at this moment.
This fence is located on the same side of Elm Street as
the Texas School Book Depository building but closer to
Stemmons Freeway. Since he is deaf, he naturally could
not hear any shots but thought he saw a puff of smoke
in the vicinity of where the two men were standing. As
soon as he saw the motorcade speed away and saw the puff of
smoke in the vicinity of the two men, the man with the
rifle looked like he was breaking the rifle down by
removing the barrel from the stock and placing it in some
dark type of suitcase that the other man was holding.
The two men then ran north on the railroad tracks by
actually running on the tracks. Hoffman was standing
approximately 75 yards from this fence. This fence was
at approximately the same height or level as the ground
.floor of the Texas School Book Depository Building.

Document 12

RE: ASSASSINATION OF PRESIDENT
     JOHN FITZGERALD KENNEDY

       .Both men were white males, both dressed in
some type of white suits, and both wore ties. He
was too far away to furnish a more detailed description.
There were no other people in his area of observation,
nor in the area where the two men were standing behind the
fence.

       On March 28, 1977, Richard H. Freeman, Texas
Instruments, Richardson, Texas, was telephonically
contacted by Special Agent ▆▆▆▆▆▆▆▆ and was requested
to contact Mr. Hoffman in an effort to communicate with
him and to advise him if he could come to the Dallas FBI
Office in order to make a personal visit to the area of
Stemmons Freeway from where he observed the presidential
motorcade on November 22, 1963.

       On March 28, 1977, Virgil E. Hoffman accompanied
Special Agent ▆▆▆▆▆▆▆▆ to Stemmons Freeway, also known
as Interstate Highway 35 North, Dallas, Texas.

       Hoffman communicated that he was driving a
1962 Ford Falcon on November 22, 1963. He parked his
car on the west shoulder of Stemmons Freeway at the
northbound lane near the Texas and Pacific Railroad overpass
that crosses Stemmons Freeway. He could not see the presidential motorcade as it was proceeding west on Elm Street
toward the Triple Underpass. He saw the motorcade speed
up as it emerged on Stemmons Freeway heading north. His
.line of vision was due east looking from Stemmons Freeway
toward the Texas School Book Depository building. The
two men he saw were behind the wooden fence above the
grassy knoll north of Elm Street and just before the
Triple Underpass. He indicated he saw smoke in that
vicinity and saw the man with the rifle disassembling the
rifle near some type of railroad track control box located
.close to the railroad tracks. Both men ran north on the

Document 13

RE: ASSASSINATION OF PRESIDENT
     JOHN FITZGERALD KENNEDY

railroad tracks.

      He tried to get the attention of a Dallas police-
man who was standing on the railroad overpass that crosses
Stemmons Freeway, but since he could not yell, he could not
communicate with the policeman. He drove his car north
on Stemmons Freeway after the motorcade passed him in an
effort to find the two men, but he lost sight of them.

      Special Agent ██████████████ took color photo-
graphs from the area of Stemmons Freeway where Mr. Hoffman
was watching the presidential motorcade on November 22,
1963. Photographs were also taken of the area north of
the grassy knoll where the wooden fence is located, and
the area adjacent to it, which is now primarily used as
a parking lot. The distance from where Mr. Hoffman was
viewing the motorcade on Stemmons Freeway to the area
behind the wooden fence is estimated at approximately 280 705
yards, with the elevation being approximately the same height
as the first floor of the Texas School Book Depository
building.

      Photographs were taken with a Bessler Topcon
camera, using Kodak Vericolor II, Type S film, with a
distance setting of infinitive, f Stop 14, and film
speed 1/125 of a second.

9*

UDO H. SPECHT

MERCANTILE CONTINENTAL BLDG.
1810 COMMERCE STREET, ROOM 200
DALLAS, TEXAS 75201
214 . 741-1851

Document 15

424 GRAND PRAIRIE ROAD
GRAND PRAIRIE, TEXAS/75050
OCTOBER 3, 1975

SEN. TED KENNEDY
WASHINGTON,D.C.

DEAR MR. KENNEDY

NOW, I WISH TO TALK YOU ABOUT YOUR BROTHER'S JOHN F. KENNEDY.
SINCE LONG TIMES AGO I REMEMBER WHAT I SAW TWO MEN RAN ON
RAILROAD FROM A FENCE. I NEVER TO FORGET A THING IN DALLAS.
I WAS SORRY, BECAUSE I AM DEAFNESS TO TALK HARD ABOUT A THING.

I TALKED F. B. I.'S OFFICE IN DALLAS LAST 1968 OR CAN'T REMEMBER
DATE AND YEAR AGO.
IF YOU WILL FIND TO SEE F.B.I.'S REPORT ABOUT I TALKED THEM.
I GUESS, MAYBE F.B.I. DID NOT KNOW UNDERSTAND WHAT I TALKED
A THING, BECAUSE I AM DEAFNESS AND HARD TO TALK F. B. I.

BUT MY UNCLE AND FATHER TOLD ME BE CAREFUL, BECAUSE IF SOMEONE
WILL HEAR WHAT I SAY THINGS FROM C.I.A. OR OTHER PERSONS OR WILL
BE VERY DANGEROUS? IF YOU THINK THIS?

IF YOU WILL HELP ME AND TELL SOME THINGS. THANK YOU MUCH.

RESPECTFULLY,

VIRGIL EDWARD HOFFMAN

Document 16

United States Senate

WASHINGTON, D.C. 20510   November 19, 1975

Mr. Virgil E. Hoffman
924 Grand Prairie Road
Grand Prairie, Texas 75050

Mr. Hoffman:

My family has been aware of various theories concerning the death of President Kennedy, just as it has been aware of the many speculative accounts which have arisen from the death of Robert Kennedy.

I am sure that it is understood that the continual speculation is painful for members of my family. We have always accepted the findings of the Warren Commission report and have no reason to question the quality and the effort of those who investigated the fatal shooting of Robert Kennedy.

Our feeling is that, if there is sufficient evidence to re-examine the circumstances concerning the deaths of President Kennedy and Robert Kennedy, this judgment would have to be made by the legal authorities responsible for such further examination. I do not believe that their judgment should be influenced by any feelings or discomfort by any member of my family.

Sincerely,

Edward M. Kennedy

Document 17

Document 18

VIRGIL E. HOFFMAN
424 Grand Prairie Road
Grand Prairie, Texas 75051-1944

October 8, 1992

Federal Bureau of Investigation   REGISTERED MAIL
1801 N. Lamar, # 300   (Return Receipt)
Dallas, Texas 75202

Attn: FOIA/PA Officer2

Dear Sir or Madame:

This is a request under the provisions of the Privacy Act of 1974
[Title 5, United States Code, Section 552a] as well as the Freedom
of Information Act (FOIA), Title 5, U.S. Code Section 552.

I hereby request a copy of any report, document, photo(s), file or
other record concerning myself, Virgil E. Hoffman, which has been
created, filed, indexed, or maintained under my name or other
personal identifier particular to me. Enclosed you will find a
signed and notarized Form DOJ-361 (Certificate of Identity)
verifying my identity.

Thank you very much for your attention to this request.

Sincerely,

Virgil E. Hoffman

Enclosure

Document 19

U.S. Department of Justice

Federal Bureau of Investigation

In Reply. Please Refer to
File No.

1801 North Lamar Suite 300
Dallas, Texas 75202
October 21, 1992

Mr. Virgil E. Hoffman
424 Grand Prairie Road
Grand Prairie, Texas 75051-1944

Dear Mr. Hoffman:

This letter is in response to your Freedom of Information - Privacy Acts (FOIPA) request dated October 8, 1992, and received by this office on October 13, 1992, concerning yourself.

A search of our indices to the central records system as maintained in the Dallas Division revealed no record responsive to your FOIPA request.

If you desire, you may submit an appeal concerning any denial contained herein. Appeals should be directed, in writing, to the Assistant Attorney General, Office of Legal Policy (ATTN: Office of Information and Privacy), United States Department of Justice, Washington, D.C. 20530. Your appeal should be submitted within 30 days from receipt of this letter. The envelope and the letter should be clearly marked "Freedom of Information Appeal" or "Information Appeal." Please cite the name of the office to which your original request was directed.

Sincerely yours,

Oliver B. Revell
Special Agent in Charge

By:

Gary L. Gerszewski
Principal Legal Advisor

Document 20

VIRGIL E. HOFFMAN
424 Grand Prairie Road
Grand Prairie, Texas 75051-1944

October 27, 1992

Federal Bureau of Investigation   CERTIFIED MAIL
FOIA/PA Branch   (Return Receipt)
Washington, DC 20535

Attn: FOIA/PA Officer

Dear Sir or Madame:

This is a request under the provisions of the Privacy Act of 1974
[Title 5, United States Code, Section 552a] as well as the Freedom
of Information Act (FOIA), Title 5, U.S. Code Section 552.

I hereby request a copy of any report, document, photo(s), file or
other record concerning myself, Virgil E. Hoffman, which has been
created, filed, indexed, or maintained under my name or other
personal identifier particular to me. Enclosed you will find a
signed and notarized Form DOJ-361 (Certificate of Identity)
verifying my identity.

In early 1977, while in my presense, FBI Agent Udo Specht made
several photographs of the area just west of the Texas School Book
Depository and just north of Elm Street in Dallas, Texas. Some of
these photos were taken of the area on Stemmons Freeway where I had
been standing on November 22, 1963 and had observed two men with
guns during President Kennedy's assassination. All of these
photographs were taken in conjuction with my testimony to Agent
Specht regarding my observations of this date. In addition to any
other information you send concerning my request, please include
8x10 color prints of these photographs.

Thank you very much for your attention to this request.

Sincerely,

Virgil E. Hoffman

Virgil E. Hoffman

Enclosure: Form DOJ-361

Document 21

Jim Marrs

P.O. Box 189, Springtown, Texas, 76082
817/433-2916

February 18, 1994

Rev. Ronald E. Friedrich
Deaf Ministries of North Texas
7611 Park Lane
Dallas TX 75225

Dear Rev. Friedrich,

Thank you for your letter of Feb. 7, dealing with Ed Hoffman and his contacts with the FBI. I have copies of Hoffman's FBI reports in my files and I too am disgruntled at the Bureau's handling of this matter.

However, it is nothing new. I can cite several instances of the FBI misquoting witnesses, to the point of making their statements the exact opposite of what they said. The Bureau, at least as far as the JFK assassination is concerned, is guilty of numerous crimes involving cover-up and obfuscation. I personally do not believe that they misunderstood Mr. Hoffman. I feel they deliberately distorted his statements, as well as amplifying and emphasizing the doubts of his parents, in an effort to discredit his testimony. His testimony, after all, went counter to the FBI's theory of the assassination.

Believing the above, I see no purpose in trying to get the FBI to correct its past mistakes. The best thing from this point on is to focus on Mr. Hoffman's story and see that it reaches the broadest possible audience. Then it won't matter much what misinformation rests in the FBI files.

Thank you so very much for your interest and help in this matter. Please pass along my best regards and well wishes to Mr. and Mrs. Hoffman.

Very truly yours,

Jim Marrs

Jim Marrs

Photo Credits
Name Index

"The shot that took the back of his head off came from some where near the west side of the book depository."

PHIL WILLIS

Photo Credits

Chapter 2
1. Googleearth
2. Jack White Collection
3. Jack White Collection
4. Jack White Collection
5. Stewart Galanor, Cover-Up
Landmark A photo: Richard Trask, "That Day in Dallas"
Landmark B photo: Ibid.

Chapter 3
All photos in the chapter courtesy of the Ed Hoffman Family

Chapter 4
6. Googleearth
7. Robert Groden Collection
8. Project JFK
9. Penn Jones, "Forgive My Grief, Volume I"
10. Googleearth
11. Mary Ferrell Collection
12. Googleearth
13. Googleearth
14. Ed Hoffman Collection
15. Ed Hoffman Collection
16. Project JFK
17. Googleearth
18. Stewart Galanor, "Cover-Up"
19. www.stationwagon.com/gallery.html
20. Ibid.
21. Jack White Collection
22. Project JFK
23. Stewart Galanor, "Cover-Up"
24. Ibid.
25. Ibid.
26. Ibid.
27. "Hearings and Exhibits, Volume 25, page 115
28. Project JFK"
29. Project JFK

30. Jack White Collection
31. Mark Lane, "Rush to Judgment" (Video)
32. Googleearth
33. Stewart Galanor, "Cover-Up"
34. Googleearth
35. Project JFK
36. Project JFK
37. www.world.guns.ru/assault.as18-e.htm
38. Richard Trask, "Pictures of the Pain" photo by Mel McIntire
39. Ibid.
40. Ibid.
41. Ibid.
42. Googleearth
43. Abraham Zapruder film
44. Jack White Collection
45. Project JFK
46. Googleearth
47. Ed Hoffman Collection
48. Project JFK
49. Ed Hoffman Collection

Chapter 7
50. Richard Trask, "Pictures of the Pain," photo by Mel McIntire
51. Ibid.
52. Robert Groden Collection
53. Project JFK
54. Jack White Collection
55. Jack White Collection
56. Mary Ferrell Collection
57. Project JFK
58. Jack White Collection
59. Jack White Collection
60. Mary Ferrell Collection
61. Mary Ferrell Collection
62. Project JFK
63. Ed Hoffman Collection
64. Robert Groden Collection
65. Ed Hoffman Collection
66. Project JFK

67. Project JFK
68. Project JFK
69. Project JFK
70. Ed Hoffman Collection
71. Project JFK
72. Project JFK
73. Project JFK
74. Jack White Collection
75. Josiah Thompson, "Six Seconds in Dallas"
76. "Hearings and Exhibits," Volume 21, page 728
77. "Hearings and Exhibits," Volume 20, page 638
78. Ibid.
79. "Hearings and Exhibits," Volume 19, page 183
80. Googleearth
81. Robert Groden, "JFK Assassination Films" (video)
82. Ibid.
83. Jack White Collection
84. Project JFK
85. Jack White Collection
86. Googleearth

Chapter 11
87. "Hearings and Exhibits," Volume 20, page 638
88. Project JFK
89. Googleearth
90. Richard Trask, "Pictures of the Pain," photo by Frank Cancellare
91. Courtesy of Harry Yardum
92. Robert Groden Collection
93. Googleearth

Chapter 12
94. Googleearth
95. Henry Hurt, "Reasonable Doubt," photo by Jim Murray
96. Ibid.
97. JFK Lancer Productions

98. "Hearings and Exhibits," Volume 20, page 162
99. "Hearings and Exhibits," Volume 20, page 160
100. Josiah Thompson, "Six Seconds in Dallas"
101. Ibid.
102. Googleearth
103. Josiah Thompson, "Six Seconds in Dallas"
104. Ibid.

Documents Section
105. Googleearth

Name Index

A
Adam, Victoria…133
Almon, John…156, 165
Altgens, James…83, 84, 87
Ames, Aldrich…110, 111
Arnold, Gordon…138, 195

B
Baker, Marrion…192
Ball, Joseph…78, 80, 86-88, 90, 92, 134, 144, 145, 151, 152, 156
Barrett, Robert…156
Bartholomew, Richard…168, 169
Batchelor, Charles…23, 45, 77
Belin, David…162-164
Bell, Mark…92-95, 101, 149
Bellah, S…45, 46, 48
Bennett, Glen…41
Bishop, Curtis…124
Bookhout, James…160
Boggs, Hale…229
Boone, Eugene…130, 149-151, 156
Bourland, Glenn…103
Bowers, Lee…28-32, 34, 92, 122, 156, 157, 166, 168, 169, 179, 190
Bradford, Clint…xii
Brehm, Charles…63
Brewer, E…45, 46
Brown, Earle…23, 24, 90-93, 96, 101, 134, 144, 145, 149, 151, 152, 187
Brown, Maggie…137, 190
Brown, Walt…141
Bugliosi, Vincent…154

C
Campbell, Ochus…127, 190
Carr, Richard…158, 159, 165-168, 179
Chism, Arthur…93
Connally, John…126, 172
Conway, Debra…xii, 157
Cooper, Roy…165, 166, 168, 179

Cooper, Sherman…149
Courtwright, Chris…165
Coswert, Ewell…124, 189
Craig, Roger…129, 158-166, 168, 179
Curry, Jesse…46, 60, 78, 80, 84, 101, 122, 123, 140

D
Decker, Bill…128-131, 158, 160, 169
Degaugh, Olan…12, 157
Dodd, Richard…124, 189
Dorman, Elsie…137, 190
Dowdy, Jim…103, 104, 194

E
Elkins, Harold…128
Ellis, S…45

F
Faulkner, Jack…131, 192
Fiester, Sherry…xii
Fischer, Ronald…135, 190
Foster, James…23, 37, 77-81, 83-88, 92, 101, 122, 123, 169, 171, 188, 189
Franzen, Jack…128, 191
Freeman, H…45, 46
Freeman, Richard…107, 108, 110, 198-200
Friedrich, Ron…xi, 57, 201
Fritz, Will…159, 160

G
Galanor, Stewart…124
Garrick, J…45, 46, 48
Gray, L…45, 46
Griffin, Will…57, 102-105, 109-112, 118, 144, 154, 184, 194-198, 200
Gotz, Earl…138

H

Haley, Earle...165
Hargis, Robert...93, 135, 170, 179, 191
Harkness, D...77, 78, 132, 192
Hartman, Wayne...137, 192
Haygood, Clyde...93, 134, 150, 151, 179
Hendrix, Annie...201
Henslee, G...46
Hickey, George...vii, 41, 44
Hill, Clint...133, 191
Hill, Jean...135, 136, 139, 191
Hoffman, Fred...106, 197
Hoffman, Frederick...16, 17, 47, 60, 106, 182
Hoffman, Robert...vii, 59-62, 106, 182
Hoffman, Rosie...xi, 19, 115, 182
Holland, Sam...38, 81-83, 123, 157, 169-170, 189
Hoover, J. Edgar...105, 111, 184, 195, 196, 229
Hudson, Emmett...127, 190
Hurt, Henry...138

J

Johnson, Clemon...125, 189
Johnson, Lyndon...4, 41, 118, 168
Jones, Penn...158, 162, 164

K

Kellerman, Roy...133, 191
Kelley, Louis...146
Kennedy, Jacqueline...40
Kennedy, Robert...118
Kennedy, Ted...57, 107, 109, 110, 118, 119, 201
Keutzer, Benjamin...160
Koumae, Dolores...127, 191

L

Lane, Mark...38
Lawrence, P...45, 146
Lawson, Winston...77
Lewis, C (Lummie)...159, 162
Lewis, Robin...xii
Lewis, Roy...138, 190

Lomax, James...23, 24, 90, 93, 96, 139, 145, 151, 152, 187
Lovelady, Billy...133, 190
Lumpkin, George...45
Lumpkin, W...45

M

Mabra, W...192
Marrs, Jim...vi, vii, xi, 4, 53, 56, 115, 116, 136, 137, 143, 144, 201
McBride, G...45, 46, 48, 49
McClellan, Robert...1
McCurley, A...131
McIntire, Mel...43, 65, 152, 153
McIntyre, William...41, 44
McKinnon, Cheryl...138, 185
McLain, Hollis...140, 192

N

Miller, Austin...125, 189
Millican, A...126
Molina, Joe...132, 190
Mooney, Luke...129
Moore, Jim...142, 149, 152
Moorman, Mary...49, 139
Morrison, Balford...171, 178
Murphy, Joe...23, 27, 85, 88, 89-91, 139, 145-149, 172, 174, 187
Murphy, Thomas...126, 189
Murray, Jim...161
Newman, Jean...127
Newman, William...21, 126, 128, 190

O

Oliver, Beverly...139, 191
Oliver, Henry...146
Oswald, Lee...vii, 2, 4, 7, 50, 62, 103, 113, 142, 159-161, 164, 169, 180, 229
Oxford, J...129

P

Paine, Michael...168
Paine, Ruth...160, 169

Bibliography

"[FBI Director J. Edgar] Hoover lied his eyes out to the [Warren] Commission. on Oswald, on Ruby, on their friends, the bullets, the gun, you name it."

CONGRESSMAN HALE BOGGS

BIBLIOGRAPHY

This bibliography lists primary sources, books, magazine articles and unpublished manuscripts used in the text. Many of the documents cited in the text were obtained by Ed Hoffman through the Freedom of Information Act and from correspondence between Ed Hoffman and other researchers.

Primary Sources

The Warren Report. Washington, D. C.; U.S. Government Printing Office, 1964.
Report on the President's Commission on the Assassination of President John F. Kennedy, Washington, D.C.; U.S. Government Printing Office, 1964.
Hearings and Exhibits Before the President's Commission on the Assassination of President John F. Kennedy. Washington, D.C.; Government Printing Office, 1964.

Secondary Sources

Bartholomew, Richard. "Possible Discovery of an Automobile Used in the JFK Conspiracy" 1993.
Benson, Michael. "Encyclopedia of the JFK Assassination" New York: Checkmark Books. 2002.
Benson, Michael. "Who's Who in the JFK Assassination" New York: Carol Publishing Group, 1993.
Brown, Walt. "Treachery in Dallas" New York: Carroll & Graf, 1995.
Brown, Walt. "Referenced Index Guide to the Warren Commission" Wilmington, Delaware: Delmax Publishing, 1995.
Bugliosi, Vincent. "Reclaiming History" New York: W. W. Norton, 2007.
Craig, Roger. "When They Kill A President" (unpublished manuscript).
Galanor, Stewart. "Cover-Up" New York: Kestrol Books, 1998.
Garrison, Jim. "On the Trail of the Assassins" New York: Warner Books, 1998.
Groden, Robert. "The Killing of a President" New York: Viking Press, 1993.
Hoffman, Ed and Friedrich, Ron. "Eye Witness" Grand Prairie, Texas: JFK Lancer Publications, 1996.
Hurt, Henry. "Reasonable Doubt" New York: Holt, Rinehart & Winston, 1985.
Marrs, Jim. "Crossfire" New York: Carroll & Graf, 1989.
Moore, Jim. "Conspiracy of One" Fort Worth: The Summit Group, 1990.
Lane, Mark. "Rush To Judgment" New York: Dell Publishing, 1966
Posner, Gerald. "Case Closed" New York: Random House, 1993.
Sloan, Bill. "Breaking the Silence" Dallas: Taylor Publishing, 1993.
Shaw, J. Gary. "Cover-up" Austin: Thomas Publications, 1976.
Sneed, Larry. "No More Silence." Dallas: Three Forks Press, 1998.
Thomas, Ralph. "The Grassy Knoll Witnesses" (unpublished manuscript)
Thomas, Ralph. "The Roger Craig Story" Austin: Thomas Investigative Publications. 1992.
Thompson, Josiah. "Six Seconds in Dallas" New York: Medallion Books, 1967.
Trask, Richard. "Pictures of the Pain" Danvers, Mass: Yeoman Press, 1994.
Trask, Richard. "That Day in Dallas" Danvers, Massachusetts: Yeoman Press, 1998.
Trask, Richard, Photographic Memory" Dallas: The Sixth Floor Museum, 1996.

Video Sources:

Antonio, Emile, director. Plot to Kill JFK: Rush to Judgment.
Story by Mark Lane. Judgment Films, 1967.
Groden, Robert. The Assassination Films. New Frontier Productions, 1994.
Turner, Nigel, director. The Men Who Killed Kennedy.
G.G. Communication Company, 1992.

Web sites:

www.maryferrell.org
www.googleearth.com
www.history-matters.com
www.aarclibrary.org
www.jfklancer.com

A Final Word

Jack White in Dealey Plaza, photo by William Reymond

Deaf people, no matter how intelligent, live their lives much differently than the rest of us. Their chief frustration is communicating their thoughts accurately. Except for those who become highly skilled at writing, they must communicate with the outside world through American Sign Language (ASL), known only by about a million people, a tiny fraction of one percent. Thus, they must depend on translations of their thoughts by others, often total strangers, of various levels of ASL comprehension. And even then, being totally deaf, they have no way of knowing whether their thoughts are being accurately relayed by the translator. Not all translators have the same degree of interpretive skill. But without any translator at all, accurate thought communication is often impossible. A subtle misinterpretation of a thought can lead to an unintended "statement."

Such was the issue faced by Ed Hoffman on November 22, 1963. Standing about 200 yards west of Dealey Plaza, he witnessed something important. He realized it must be very important after he saw the bloody body of the slain President pass below his elevated position on Stemmons Freeway.

Being deaf, most mutes depend on their other senses to help compensate for their hearing loss. They observe things a hearing person might miss. And that day, Ed Hoffman saw something horrible. Then he realized that just moments before, he had witnessed a highly unusual event which *must* be connected to the murder he had just observed.

He tried to tell the authorities what he had seen. He was an eyewitness and he wanted to help. Although he told his story to many people, most did not understand. Nobody had the ability or the patience to learn his story except close family members. His family was concerned for his safety and felt obligated to protect him. It seemed to Ed Hoffman that nobody cared about what he saw that day.

But in Brian Edwards and Casey Quinlan, Ed finally found the investigators who took the time to dig into Ed's story and to ensure that his account was accurately preserved for the sake of historical accuracy and truth.

This book finally tells Ed's story, accurately and honestly. Now, after nearly forty-five years after the event, Ed can rest easy. His account as he lived it has finally been recorded. Ed is a true patriot who persevered until he made someone understand. I hope you will understand too, thanks to Brian and Casey.

Jack White

Printed in the USA
CPSIA information can be obtained
at www.ICGtesting.com
CBHW080737280724
12235CB00020B/443